Colorado Real Est

Colorado Real Estate License Exam: Best Test Prep Book to Help You Get Your License!

The Ultimate Workbook: Salesperson and Broker Exam-Passing Strategies

Table of Content

Introduction

If you're holding this book, chances are you're either considering or have already decided to embark on a rewarding career in real estate, specifically in the beautiful state of Colorado. First and foremost, congratulations! The path you're about to tread offers not just financial rewards but also the opportunity to help people realize their dreams of home ownership, investment, and more. This book aims to be your comprehensive guide, your go-to resource, as you navigate the complexities of the Colorado real estate industry, starting with acing the Colorado Real Estate License Exam.

Why Colorado?

Colorado is more than just a state; it's a state of mind. With its diverse landscapes, ranging from arid deserts to snowy mountain peaks, Colorado offers a unique backdrop for real estate professionals. The state has seen significant growth in recent years, making it a hot market for real estate. Whether you're interested in residential, commercial, or rural real estate, Colorado has something for everyone. This book will delve into the specifics of the Colorado real estate market, providing localized insights that generic real estate guides can't offer.

What This Book Offers

Comprehensive Coverage

This book is designed to be a one-stop-shop for all your Colorado real estate exam preparation needs. It covers a wide range of topics, from the fundamentals of real estate to Colorado-specific laws and regulations. Each chapter is crafted to provide in-depth knowledge, practical tips, and actionable advice.

Mock Exams and Practice Questions

One of the best ways to prepare for any exam is to practice, practice, practice. This book includes mock exams and practice questions tailored to the Colorado Real Estate License Exam, allowing you to test your knowledge and improve your test-taking skills.

Real-World Insights

Beyond just helping you pass an exam, this book aims to prepare you for a successful career in Colorado real estate. It includes chapters on career development, ethical considerations, and even day-to-day tips for once you've obtained your license.

Who Should Read This Book?

Whether you're a complete novice to the world of real estate or a seasoned professional looking to transition to the Colorado market, this book is for you. It's designed to cater to a wide audience, including:

- Aspiring real estate agents
- Current agents looking to move to Colorado
- Real estate investors interested in the Colorado market
- Anybody curious about the intricacies of Colorado real estate

Your Journey Starts Here

As you turn the pages of this book, you're not just reading; you're taking actionable steps toward a brighter future in Colorado real estate. Each chapter is a milestone on your journey, and by the end, you'll be well-equipped to take the Colorado Real Estate License Exam and kickstart your career.

So, let's get started. Your future in Colorado real estate awaits, and this book is your first step toward realizing it.

Understanding the Colorado Real Estate Market

The Colorado real estate market is as diverse as its landscapes, offering a range of opportunities for both buyers and sellers. Understanding this market is crucial for anyone aspiring to succeed in Colorado's real estate industry. This chapter aims to provide a comprehensive overview of the Colorado real estate market, covering key aspects such as market trends, property types, and regional variations.

Market Trends

Population Growth

Colorado has experienced significant population growth in recent years, particularly in cities like Denver, Colorado Springs, and Boulder. This growth has led to increased demand for housing and commercial spaces.

Economic Factors

Colorado's strong economy, driven by sectors like technology, renewable energy, and tourism, has a direct impact on the real estate market. A robust economy generally leads to higher property values.

Seasonal Variations

The real estate market in Colorado is subject to seasonal variations. For example, mountain properties may see increased interest during ski season, while beachfront properties may be more popular in the summer.

Property Types

Residential Properties

From single-family homes to luxury estates, the residential market in Colorado is diverse. Suburban areas offer larger homes with yards, while urban areas like downtown Denver offer condos and apartments.

Commercial Properties

The commercial market includes office spaces, retail locations, and industrial properties. Cities like Denver and Boulder have thriving commercial markets due to their strong economies.

Rural and Recreational Properties

Colorado's diverse landscapes offer various opportunities for rural and recreational properties, including farms, ranches, and vacation homes.

Regional Variations

Front Range

The Front Range, which includes cities like Denver, Colorado Springs, and Fort Collins, is the most populous region and has the most active real estate market.

Western Slope

The Western Slope is known for its natural beauty, attracting buyers interested in recreational properties.

Eastern Plains

The Eastern Plains offer more affordable options and are ideal for those looking for rural properties.

Financing and Investment

Mortgage Trends

Understanding mortgage rates and lending practices in Colorado can help you guide your clients through the buying process.

Investment Opportunities

Colorado's strong economy and population growth make it an attractive location for real estate investment, both for rental properties and property flipping.

Legal and Regulatory Environment

Property Taxes

Colorado has unique property tax laws that vary by county. Understanding these can help you provide better advice to your clients.

Zoning Laws

Zoning laws in Colorado can affect property usage, so it's crucial to understand these when advising clients.

Challenges and Opportunities

Housing Affordability

Rising property values have led to concerns about housing affordability, particularly in rapidly growing cities.

Sustainability

Colorado is at the forefront of sustainable living, and properties with eco-friendly features can command higher prices.

Conclusion

Understanding the Colorado real estate market is crucial for success in this industry. From market trends to property types and regional variations, this chapter has aimed to provide a comprehensive overview to equip you with the knowledge you need.

Action Steps for the Reader

1. Research current market trends in your area of interest within Colorado.

2. Familiarize yourself with the legal and regulatory environment, including property taxes and zoning laws.

3. Consider specializing in a particular type of property or region to become an expert in that niche.

By gaining a deep understanding of the Colorado real estate market, you'll be better equipped to serve your clients and succeed in your career.

Eligibility Criteria

Becoming a licensed real estate agent in Colorado is a multi-step process that begins with meeting specific eligibility criteria. This chapter aims to provide a comprehensive guide to understanding the qualifications, prerequisites, and other requirements you'll need to fulfill to start your journey in Colorado's real estate industry.

Basic Requirements

Age and Citizenship

You must be at least 18 years old and a U.S. citizen or lawfully admitted alien to apply for a real estate license in Colorado.

Background Check

A thorough background check is conducted to ensure that you have no disqualifying criminal history. This usually involves fingerprinting and an FBI criminal background check.

Educational Qualifications

A high school diploma or its equivalent is generally required. Some brokerages may prefer candidates with a college degree, although it's not a state requirement.

Pre-Licensing Education

Required Hours

Colorado requires aspiring real estate agents to complete 168 hours of pre-licensing education from an accredited institution.

Course Content

The courses cover a variety of topics, including Colorado real estate law, contract law, and principles of real estate.

Exam Preparation

Many pre-licensing courses also offer exam preparation modules, including practice tests and study materials.

Application Process

Documentation

You'll need to provide various documents, including proof of identity, educational certificates, and background check results.

Fees

There is an application fee that you'll need to pay when submitting your application, which is non-refundable.

Online vs. Paper Application

Colorado allows for both online and paper applications, although online is generally faster and more convenient.

State Exam

Exam Format

The Colorado Real Estate License Exam is divided into a national portion and a state-specific portion.

Passing Score

You must achieve a passing score on both portions of the exam to qualify for a license.

Exam Centers

The exam is administered at various testing centers across Colorado, and you'll need to schedule your exam in advance.

Post-Exam Requirements

Errors and Omissions Insurance

After passing the exam, you'll need to obtain Errors and Omissions (E&O) insurance, which protects you against liability.

Broker Affiliation

You must be affiliated with a licensed Colorado broker to activate your real estate license.

License Activation

Once you've met all post-exam requirements, you can officially activate your license and begin practicing.

Special Cases

Reciprocity

Colorado has reciprocity agreements with some states, allowing licensed agents from those states to become licensed in Colorado more easily.

Disqualifying Factors

Certain criminal convictions or disciplinary actions in other states may disqualify you from obtaining a license in Colorado.

Renewal and Continuing Education

Renewal Period

Colorado real estate licenses must be renewed every three years.

Continuing Education

You'll need to complete 24 hours of continuing education during each renewal period to maintain your license.

Conclusion

Meeting the eligibility criteria is the first crucial step in becoming a licensed real estate agent in Colorado. From basic requirements to educational qualifications and post-exam steps, this chapter has aimed to provide a comprehensive guide to help you understand what you need to become eligible for a real estate license in Colorado.

Action Steps for the Reader

1. Verify that you meet the basic age and citizenship requirements.
2. Start researching accredited institutions for your pre-licensing education.

3. Gather all necessary documents for the application process.

By understanding and fulfilling these eligibility criteria, you'll be well on your way to launching a successful career in Colorado's real estate industry.

Application Process

The application process for obtaining a real estate license in Colorado is a structured, multi-step journey that requires careful planning and attention to detail. This chapter aims to provide a comprehensive guide to navigating this process, from initial preparations to the final steps of license activation.

Initial Preparations

Research and Planning

Before you start the application process, it's crucial to research the requirements and timelines. Create a checklist and a timeline to keep track of your progress.

Budgeting

There are various fees associated with the application process, including course fees, exam fees, and application fees. Budgeting in advance can help you manage your finances effectively.

Selecting a Pre-Licensing School

Colorado requires 168 hours of pre-licensing education. Choose an accredited school that fits your learning style, whether it's online or in-person.

Pre-Licensing Education

Enrollment

Once you've selected a school, the next step is enrollment. This usually involves submitting an application form and paying a course fee.

Course Completion

You must complete the required 168 hours of education, which covers topics like Colorado real estate law, contract law, and principles of real estate.

Course Exam

Most pre-licensing courses have a final exam. You must pass this exam to receive your course completion certificate, which you'll need for the state exam.

Background Check and Fingerprints

Scheduling

After completing your pre-licensing education, schedule your fingerprinting appointment. Colorado requires a criminal background check for all real estate license applicants.

Results

The background check results are usually sent directly to the Colorado Real Estate Commission. Make sure to follow up to confirm they've received it.

State Exam Registration

Scheduling

You can schedule your state exam online or by phone. Make sure to do this well in advance, as slots can fill up quickly.

Exam Fee

There is a fee for the state exam, which is usually payable online or over the phone when you schedule your exam.

Preparing for the Exam

Use the time leading up to the exam for focused study and review. Many applicants find it helpful to take practice exams during this period.

Taking the State Exam

On the Day

Arrive early at the exam center with all required identification. Follow all rules and guidelines provided by the exam administrators.

Exam Results

You'll receive your exam results immediately upon completion. If you pass, you'll receive a certificate of passing, which is required for the next steps.

License Application

Online Application

Colorado allows for online license applications, which is the fastest and most convenient method.

Required Documents

You'll need to upload various documents, including your course completion certificate, background check results, and proof of age and citizenship.

Application Fee

There is a non-refundable application fee that you'll need to pay when submitting your application.

Post-Application Steps

Errors and Omissions Insurance

After your application is approved, you'll need to obtain Errors and Omissions (E&O) insurance.

Broker Affiliation

You must be affiliated with a licensed Colorado broker to activate your license.

License Activation

Once all post-application requirements are met, you can activate your license and begin practicing.

Conclusion

The application process for a Colorado real estate license is comprehensive but manageable if approached with careful planning and attention to detail. This chapter has aimed to provide a step-by-step guide to help you navigate this process successfully.

Action Steps for the Reader

1. Create a checklist and timeline for the application process.
2. Budget for all associated fees.
3. Begin your pre-licensing education and plan for the state exam.

Exam Format

The Colorado Real Estate License Exam is a critical milestone on your path to becoming a licensed real estate agent in the state. Understanding the exam format is crucial for effective preparation and ultimately, for passing the exam. This chapter aims to provide a comprehensive guide to the exam's structure, types of questions, scoring, and strategies for success.

Overview of the Exam

Components

The exam is divided into two main components: the National portion and the State portion. Both are designed to test your knowledge and understanding of real estate principles, laws, and practices.

Duration

The total time allocated for the exam is approximately 4 hours, with each portion taking about 2 hours.

Number of Questions

The National portion typically consists of 80 multiple-choice questions, while the State portion has around 74.

Passing Score

The passing score for each portion is usually around 75%, but this can vary slightly.

Types of Questions

Recall Questions

These questions test your ability to recall facts and figures, such as definitions or real estate laws.

Application Questions

These questions require you to apply your knowledge to specific scenarios. For example, you may be asked to identify the correct course of action in a given situation.

Analysis Questions

These are the most complex type of questions, requiring you to analyze information, draw conclusions, and make judgments.

National Portion

Topics Covered

- Property Ownership
- Land Use Controls and Regulations
- Valuation and Market Analysis
- Financing
- General Principles of Agency
- Property Disclosures

Question Distribution

The questions in the National portion are usually evenly distributed among the topics, although this can vary.

State Portion

Topics Covered

- Colorado Real Estate Commission Rules and Regulations
- Colorado Contracts and Regulations
- Colorado Statutes Affecting Real Estate
- Closing and Settlement Costs

Question Distribution

The State portion focuses heavily on Colorado-specific laws and regulations, so expect a higher concentration of questions on these topics.

Scoring and Results

Instant Results

You will receive your exam results immediately upon completion. If you pass, you'll receive a certificate of passing, which is required for the next steps in the licensing process.

Failing the Exam

If you fail one or both portions of the exam, you'll receive a diagnostic report indicating your performance in each subject area. This can be a valuable tool for targeted studying before retaking the exam.

Exam Day Tips

What to Bring

You'll need to bring government-issued photo identification, your exam confirmation number, and any other materials specified by the exam center.

What Not to Bring

Most exam centers prohibit bringing personal items like bags, phones, or notes into the exam room.

Time Management

Time management is crucial. Consider allocating a specific amount of time to each question and keeping an eye on the clock.

Strategies for Success

Practice Exams

Taking practice exams can help you become familiar with the question format and improve your time management skills.

Study Groups

Joining a study group can provide additional perspectives and help you cover more material.

Rest and Relaxation

Make sure to get a good night's sleep before the exam and try relaxation techniques to reduce anxiety.

Conclusion

Understanding the format of the Colorado Real Estate License Exam is crucial for effective preparation and success. This chapter has aimed to provide a comprehensive guide to help you navigate the exam confidently.

Action Steps for the Reader

1. Familiarize yourself with the types of questions and topics covered in both the National and State portions.

2. Take practice exams to assess your readiness.

3. Develop a study plan based on your strengths and weaknesses.

By understanding the exam format and preparing accordingly, you're well on your way to passing the Colorado Real Estate License Exam and starting your career in real estate.

Property Ownership and Land Use Controls

Understanding property ownership and land use controls is a cornerstone of real estate practice. This chapter aims to provide a comprehensive guide to these topics, focusing on the Colorado context. From types of property ownership to zoning laws and environmental regulations, this chapter will equip you with the knowledge you need to navigate Colorado's real estate landscape.

Types of Property Ownership

Fee Simple Absolute

This is the most complete form of ownership, where the owner has full control over the property, subject only to public and private restrictions like zoning laws and covenants.

Life Estate

In a life estate, ownership of the property is for the duration of someone's life, usually the life tenant. Upon their death, the property reverts to a designated remainderman.

Leasehold Estate

Here, the tenant has the right to use and possess the property for a specific period, as defined in the lease agreement.

Joint Tenancy

In a joint tenancy, two or more people own property with the right of survivorship, meaning if one owner dies, their share is distributed among the surviving owners.

Tenancy in Common

Unlike joint tenancy, there is no right of survivorship. Each owner can sell or transfer their share independently.

Community Property

This is a form of ownership between married persons where most property acquired during the marriage is owned jointly.

Land Use Controls

Zoning Laws

Zoning laws regulate how land can be used in different areas, known as zones. For example, residential, commercial, and industrial are common zoning categories.

Variances and Rezoning

Sometimes, property owners can apply for a variance to use their property in a way that is not typically allowed by zoning laws. Rezoning is a more permanent change but is harder to achieve.

Building Codes

These are sets of rules that specify the minimum acceptable levels of safety for constructed objects such as buildings.

Environmental Regulations

Colorado has specific environmental regulations to protect natural resources. These can affect land use, especially in areas near water bodies or protected lands.

Historic Preservation

Some areas in Colorado are designated as historic districts, and there are restrictions on what can be done to properties in these areas.

Homeowners Associations (HOAs)

HOAs often have their own sets of rules and regulations that affect land use, from the color you can paint your house to the types of plants you can have in your yard.

Easements and Encroachments

Easements

An easement is the right to use someone else's land for a specific purpose, like a driveway or utility lines.

Encroachments

An encroachment occurs when a building or some portion of it intrudes onto a neighboring property.

Colorado-Specific Considerations

Water Rights

In Colorado, water rights are a significant concern and are separate from land ownership. The prior appropriation system is used, meaning "first in time, first in right."

Mineral Rights

Colorado has abundant natural resources, and mineral rights can be a complicated issue, often separated from surface property rights.

Agricultural Land

Special rules apply to agricultural land, including tax incentives and easements for conservation.

Tax Implications

Property Taxes

Property taxes in Colorado are based on the assessed value of the property and can vary significantly depending on the location and use of the land.

Capital Gains Tax

When selling property, you may be subject to capital gains tax on any profit you make.

Conclusion

Understanding property ownership and land use controls is crucial for anyone involved in Colorado's real estate industry. This chapter has aimed to provide a comprehensive overview of these topics, from the types of property ownership to the various controls and regulations that affect how land can be used in Colorado.

Action Steps for the Reader

1. Familiarize yourself with the zoning laws in your area of interest.
2. Understand the different types of property ownership and their implications.
3. Be aware of any environmental or historical regulations that could affect your property.

Mock Exam Property Ownership and Land Use Controls

➡1. What is the most complete form of ownership?

    A. Life Estate

    B. Leasehold Estate

    C. Fee Simple Absolute

    D. Joint Tenancy

Answer: C. Fee Simple Absolute

Fee Simple Absolute grants the owner all rights to the property, including the ability to sell, lease, or will it to heirs.

➡2. What does a life estate provide?

    A. Complete control of the property

    B. Ownership for the duration of someone's life

    C. Equal ownership among spouses

    D. Ownership for a specified period

Answer: B. Ownership for the duration of someone's life

A life estate grants ownership for the duration of someone's life, usually the life tenant. Upon their death, the property reverts to the original owner or a designated remainderman.

➡3. What is the primary advantage of a Leasehold Estate?

    A. Equity build-up

    B. Lower upfront costs

    C. Complete control

    D. Right of survivorship

Answer: B. Lower upfront costs

The primary advantage of a Leasehold Estate is lower upfront costs. The tenant has the right to occupy and use the property for a specified period, but ownership remains with the landlord.

➡4. What is unique about Joint Tenancy?

    A. Unequal shares

    B. No right of survivorship

    C. Equal shares and right of survivorship

    D. Complete control of the property

Answer: C. Equal shares and right of survivorship

Joint tenancy involves two or more people owning property with equal shares and the right of survivorship.

➡5. In which states is Community Property a common form of ownership?

    A. All states

    B. Only in community property states

    C. Only in common law states

    D. None of the above

Answer: B. Only in community property states

Community Property is a form of ownership common in community property states, where any property acquired during a marriage is considered jointly owned by both spouses.

➡6. What is the primary purpose of zoning laws?

    A. To control property taxes

    B. To regulate land use

C. To establish school districts

D. To determine property value

Answer: B. To regulate land use

Zoning laws are enacted by local governments to regulate how land can be used in specific areas.

➡ **7. What is eminent domain?**

A. The right to lease property

B. The right of the government to take private property for public use

C. The right to inherit property

D. The right to sell property

Answer: B. The right of the government to take private property for public use

Eminent domain is the power of the government to take private property for public use, usually with compensation to the owner.

➡ **8. What is a variance in the context of land use?**

A. A change in property value

B. A change in zoning laws

C. Permission to use land in a way that is prohibited by zoning laws

D. A change in property taxes

Answer: C. Permission to use land in a way that is prohibited by zoning laws

A variance is special permission granted by a zoning authority to use land in a manner that is generally not allowed under current zoning laws.

➡ **9. What is a restrictive covenant?**

A. A government-imposed restriction on land use

B. A privately imposed agreement that restricts the use of land

C. A restriction on the sale of property

D. A restriction on leasing property

Answer: B. A privately imposed agreement that restricts the use of land

A restrictive covenant is an agreement that limits how a property owner can use their property, usually to preserve the value and integrity of a neighborhood.

➡ **10. What is the difference between real property and personal property?**

A. Real property can be moved, but personal property cannot

B. Real property is land and anything permanently attached to it, while personal property is movable

C. Real property is always more valuable

D. There is no difference

Answer: B. Real property is land and anything permanently attached to it, while personal property is movable

Real property refers to land and anything permanently attached to it, like buildings. Personal property refers to movable items like furniture and cars.

➡ **11. What is a buffer zone in land use planning?**

A. An area between residential and commercial zones

B. An area reserved for parks

C. An area where any type of construction is allowed

D. An area reserved for schools

Answer: A. An area between residential and commercial zones

A buffer zone is an area that separates different types of land uses, like residential and commercial, to reduce conflict between them.

➡️12. What is the main goal of sustainable development?

   A. To maximize profits

   B. To use resources in a way that meets current needs without compromising future needs

   C. To develop as quickly as possible

   D. To use all available land

Answer: B. To use resources in a way that meets current needs without compromising future needs

Sustainable development aims to meet the needs of the present without compromising the ability of future generations to meet their own needs.

➡️13. What is a master plan in the context of city planning?

   A. A detailed budget

   B. A long-term planning document that guides future growth and development

   C. A short-term plan for immediate construction

   D. A plan for a single building

Answer: B. A long-term planning document that guides future growth and development

A master plan is a comprehensive long-term plan that outlines the vision, policies, and goals for future growth and development in a city or community.

➡️14. What is the main purpose of a building permit?

   A. To raise revenue for the city

   B. To ensure that construction complies with local codes and ordinances

   C. To limit the number of buildings in an area

   D. To increase property values

Answer: B. To ensure that construction complies with local codes and ordinances

A building permit is required to ensure that any new construction or significant changes to existing structures comply with local building codes and regulations.

→ **15. What is the role of a property appraiser in land use?**

    A. To determine the highest and best use of a property

    B. To enforce zoning laws

    C. To issue building permits

    D. To draft master plans

Answer: A. To determine the highest and best use of a property

A property appraiser assesses the value of a property based on its highest and best use, considering factors like location, zoning, and market conditions.

→ **16. What is the "Right to Farm" law?**

    A. A law that allows anyone to farm anywhere

    B. A law that protects farmers from nuisance lawsuits

    C. A law that restricts farming to certain zones

    D. A law that bans farming in urban areas

Answer: B. A law that protects farmers from nuisance lawsuits

The "Right to Farm" law is designed to protect existing farmers from nuisance lawsuits filed by new neighbors who may not be accustomed to the operations of a farm.

→ **17. What does the term "infill development" refer to?**

    A. Developing farmland into residential areas

    B. Developing open spaces in urban areas

    C. Developing new structures on vacant or underused land within existing city boundaries

    D. Expanding urban areas into rural zones

Answer: C. Developing new structures on vacant or underused land within existing city boundaries

Infill development aims to make use of vacant or underutilized lands within a built-up area for further construction or development.

➠18. What is a nonconforming use?

A. A use that conforms to current zoning laws but not to building codes

B. A use that was lawful before a zoning ordinance was passed but is no longer permitted

C. A use that violates both zoning laws and building codes

D. A use that is temporarily permitted due to a variance

Answer: B. A use that was lawful before a zoning ordinance was passed but is no longer permitted

A nonconforming use is a land use that was legal when established but does not conform to new or changed zoning laws.

➠19. What is the main purpose of a land trust?

A. To hold land for development

B. To preserve land for future generations

C. To generate revenue through land sales

D. To control land prices

Answer: B. To preserve land for future generations

A land trust is an organization that actively works to conserve land by undertaking or assisting in land or conservation easement acquisition.

➠20. What is "mixed-use development"?

A. Development that includes both residential and commercial properties

B. Development that is used for industrial purposes

C. Development that is only used for residential purposes

D. Development that is only used for commercial purposes

Answer: A. Development that includes both residential and commercial properties

Mixed-use development is a type of urban development that blends residential, commercial, cultural, institutional, or entertainment uses.

➡ **21. What is the primary purpose of a greenbelt?**

A. To provide recreational spaces

B. To separate urban areas from rural areas

C. To increase property values

D. To reduce air pollution

Answer: B. To separate urban areas from rural areas

A greenbelt is an area of largely undeveloped, wild, or agricultural land surrounding or neighboring urban areas.

➡ **22. What is "brownfield land"?**

A. Land that is used for agricultural purposes

B. Land that has been contaminated by hazardous waste

C. Land that is reserved for parks and recreation

D. Land that is zoned for industrial use

Answer: B. Land that has been contaminated by hazardous waste

Brownfield land is a term used in urban planning to describe any previously developed land that is not currently in use and may be potentially contaminated.

➡ **23. What does "highest and best use" mean in the context of real estate?**

A. The use that generates the most income

B. The use that is most suitable from a social perspective

C. The use that maximizes a property's value

D. The use that is most environmentally sustainable

Answer: C. The use that maximizes a property's value

"Highest and best use" is a real estate appraisal term for the most profitable, likely use of a property, which is physically possible, appropriately supported, and legally permissible.

➞**24. What is "air rights"?**

A. The right to unlimited views from a property

B. The right to the air above the land

C. The right to pollute the air

D. The right to fresh air

Answer: B. The right to the air above the land

Air rights are a type of development right in real estate, referring to the empty space above a property.

➞**25. What is "land banking"?**

A. The process of buying land as an investment

B. The process of rezoning land

C. The process of converting agricultural land to residential land

D. The process of accumulating land for future development

Answer: D. The process of accumulating land for future development

Land banking is the practice of aggregating parcels of land for future sale or development.

➞**26. What is "eminent domain"?**

A. The right of the government to tax property

B. The right of the government to seize private property for public use

C. The right of the property owner to change the zoning laws

D. The right of the property owner to deny access to government officials

Answer: B. The right of the government to seize private property for public use

Eminent domain is the power of the government to take private property and convert it into public use, often with compensation to the owner.

➡ 27. What is "spot zoning"?

A. Zoning that changes frequently

B. Zoning that applies to a specific area within a larger zoned area

C. Zoning that applies only to commercial properties

D. Zoning that applies only during certain times of the year

Answer: B. Zoning that applies to a specific area within a larger zoned area

Spot zoning is the application of zoning laws that are different from the surrounding area, usually benefiting a single property owner.

➡ 28. What does "buffer zone" mean in the context of land use?

A. An area that separates different types of land uses

B. An area that is restricted for military use

C. An area that is designated for future development

D. An area that is kept empty for aesthetic purposes

Answer: A. An area that separates different types of land uses

A buffer zone is a zonal area that lies between two or more other areas that are contrasting in nature.

➡ 29. What is "downzoning"?

A. Changing the zoning of a property to a less intensive use

B. Changing the zoning of a property to a more intensive use

C. Rezoning to allow for higher buildings

D. Rezoning to allow for commercial use

Answer: A. Changing the zoning of a property to a less intensive use

Downzoning is the rezoning of land to a more restrictive zone to prevent overdevelopment.

➡30. What is "land grading"?

A. The process of making land more level

B. The process of evaluating the quality of soil

C. The process of determining the value of the land

D. The process of rezoning land

Answer: A. The process of making land more level

Land grading is the act of leveling the surface of the soil to prepare it for construction or agriculture.

➡31. What is "land reclamation"?

A. The process of converting developed land back to its natural state

B. The process of converting barren land into arable land

C. The process of restoring contaminated land

D. All of the above

Answer: D. All of the above

Land reclamation can involve converting barren land into arable land, restoring contaminated land, or converting developed land back to its natural state.

➡32. What is "land tenure"?

A. The legal regime in which land is owned

B. The length of time land has been owned by a single entity

C. The tax status of a piece of land

D. The zoning classification of a piece of land

Answer: A. The legal regime in which land is owned

Land tenure is the way land is held or owned at the individual or collective level.

➠33. What is "land partition"?

A. The division of a larger piece of land into smaller lots

B. The legal process to settle land disputes

C. The change of land zoning types

D. The process of land reclamation

Answer: A. The division of a larger piece of land into smaller lots

Land partition is the division of real property into two or more parcels.

➠34. What is "land speculation"?

A. Buying land with the hope that its value will increase

B. Buying land for immediate development

C. Buying land for long-term investment

D. Buying land for agricultural use

Answer: A. Buying land with the hope that its value will increase

Land speculation is the purchase of land with the hope that it will increase in value for resale at a profit.

➠35. What is "land surveying"?

A. The process of measuring land and its features

B. The process of evaluating the quality of soil

C. The process of determining the value of the land

D. The process of rezoning land

Answer: A. The process of measuring land and its features

Land surveying is the technique of determining the terrestrial or three-dimensional position of points and the distances and angles between them.

➡**36. What is "inclusionary zoning"?**

A. Zoning that includes only residential properties

B. Zoning that mandates a portion of new development be affordable for low-income households

C. Zoning that includes only commercial properties

D. Zoning that includes only industrial properties

Answer: B. Zoning that mandates a portion of new development be affordable for low-income households

Inclusionary zoning is a regulation that requires a given share of new construction to be affordable for people with low to moderate incomes.

➡**37. What is "land banking"?**

A. The process of buying land for immediate development

B. The process of holding onto land as a long-term investment

C. The process of using land as collateral for a loan

D. The process of converting barren land into arable land

Answer: B. The process of holding onto land as a long-term investment

Land banking is the practice of aggregating parcels of land for future sale or development.

➡**38. What does "air rights" refer to?**

A. The right to unlimited height in building above a property

B. The right to clean air in a residential area

C. The right to the airspace above the physical property

D. The right to fly drones over a property

Answer: C. The right to the airspace above the physical property

Air rights are the property interest in the "space" above the earth's surface.

➡ **39. What is "land assembly"?**

A. The process of gathering various small parcels of land into a single larger parcel

B. The process of constructing a building on a piece of land

C. The process of converting barren land into arable land

D. The process of dividing a larger piece of land into smaller lots

Answer: A. The process of gathering various small parcels of land into a single larger parcel

Land assembly is the process by which smaller parcels of land are combined to create a single larger parcel.

➡ **40. What is "land degradation"?**

A. The process of land losing its productivity due to human activities

B. The process of land increasing in value

C. The process of land being rezoned for less intensive use

D. The process of land being converted into a natural reserve

Answer: A. The process of land losing its productivity due to human activities

Land degradation refers to the deterioration or loss of the productive capacity of the soils for present and future.

➡ **41. What is "land improvement"?**

A. The process of adding value to a land through developments like roads and utilities

B. The process of converting barren land into arable land

C. The process of rezoning land for more intensive use

D. The process of restoring contaminated land

Answer: A. The process of adding value to a land through developments like roads and utilities

Land improvement refers to the effort made to make land more usable and valuable.

➡️**42. What is "land lease"?**

A. A contract where the landowner gives another the right to use land in exchange for rent

B. A contract to sell land

C. A contract to buy land

D. A contract to develop land

Answer: A. A contract where the landowner gives another the right to use land in exchange for rent

A land lease is an agreement where the landowner permits a tenant to use the land in exchange for rent.

➡️**43. What is "land reservation"?**

A. Land set aside for future use

B. Land set aside for indigenous people

C. Land set aside for environmental protection

D. All of the above

Answer: D. All of the above

Land reservation can refer to land set aside for various purposes, including future use, protection of indigenous rights, or environmental conservation.

➡44. What is "land trust"?

A. A legal entity that holds the ownership of a land for the benefit of another party

B. A company that invests in land

C. A non-profit organization that protects land for future generations

D. A government agency that manages public lands

Answer: A. A legal entity that holds the ownership of a land for the benefit of another party

A land trust is a legal entity that takes ownership of, or authority over, a property at the behest of the property owner.

➡45. What is "land use planning"?

A. The process of managing land resources to prevent land degradation

B. The process of determining the best way to use land resources

C. The process of rezoning land

D. The process of converting barren land into arable land

Answer: B. The process of determining the best way to use land resources

Land use planning involves the systematic assessment of land and water potential, alternatives for land use, and the economic and social conditions.

➡46. What does "eminent domain" refer to?

A. The right of the government to take private property for public use

B. The right of a landlord to evict a tenant for non-payment of rent

C. The right of a property owner to develop their land as they see fit

D. The right of a tenant to enjoy their rented property without interference from the landlord

Answer: A. The right of the government to take private property for public use

Eminent domain is the power of the government to take private property and convert it into public use, usually with compensation to the owner.

➡47. What is "adverse possession"?

A. The illegal occupation of property

B. The acquisition of property through inheritance

C. The acquisition of property through a long-term, open, and notorious occupation

D. The acquisition of property through a legal purchase

Answer: C. The acquisition of property through a long-term, open, and notorious occupation

Adverse possession is a legal principle that allows a person who possesses someone else's land for an extended period of time to claim legal title to that land.

➡48. What is "land value tax"?

A. A tax on the value of a building

B. A tax on the value of land, excluding the value of buildings and improvements

C. A tax on the sale of land

D. A tax on the rental income from land

Answer: B. A tax on the value of land, excluding the value of buildings and improvements

A land value tax is a levy on the unimproved value of land.

➡49. What is "landlocked property"?

A. Property that is surrounded by other properties, with no direct access to a public road

B. Property that is located far from any body of water

C. Property that is not subject to flooding

D. Property that is restricted from development

Answer: A. Property that is surrounded by other properties, with no direct access to a public road

Landlocked property is real estate that has no direct access to a public street, so you can't get to it unless you go through someone else's property first.

→50. What is "latent defect"?

A. A defect that is obvious and easy to spot

B. A defect that is hidden and not immediately obvious

C. A defect that has been disclosed by the seller

D. A defect that has been repaired before the sale of the property

Answer: B. A defect that is hidden and not immediately obvious

A latent defect is a fault in the property that could not have been discovered by a reasonably thorough inspection before the sale.

Laws of Agency and Fiduciary Duties

Understanding the laws of agency and fiduciary duties is crucial for anyone entering the real estate profession in Colorado. This chapter aims to provide a comprehensive guide on these topics, including the legal obligations and ethical standards that govern the relationships between agents, clients, and third parties.

The Concept of Agency

Definition

Agency in real estate refers to the relationship between a real estate agent and their client, where the agent represents the client in property transactions.

Creation of Agency

Agency can be created through express agreements, like a listing agreement for sellers or a buyer's agency agreement for buyers. It can also be implied through the actions of the parties.

Types of Agency

Seller's Agent

Represents the seller in a transaction and owes fiduciary duties to the seller.

Buyer's Agent

Represents the buyer in a transaction and owes fiduciary duties to the buyer.

Dual Agency

Represents both the buyer and the seller in a transaction. This is legal in Colorado but requires informed consent from both parties.

Transaction Broker

A transaction broker assists both parties without being an agent for either. This is common in Colorado.

Fiduciary Duties

Definition

Fiduciary duties are the legal obligations that an agent owes to their client. They are the highest duties known to the law.

Types of Fiduciary Duties

Loyalty

The agent must act in the best interest of their client, even above their own interests.

Confidentiality

The agent must keep all confidential information about the client private unless required by law to disclose it.

Disclosure

The agent must disclose all material facts known to them that could affect the client's decision-making.

Obedience

The agent must follow all lawful instructions from the client.

Reasonable Care and Diligence

The agent must exercise reasonable care in performing their duties, including staying informed about market conditions.

Accounting

The agent must account for all money and property received during the transaction.

Colorado-Specific Laws and Regulations

Brokerage Relationship Agreements

In Colorado, the brokerage relationship must be defined in writing, usually through a "Brokerage Disclosure to Buyer" or "Brokerage Disclosure to Seller" form.

Vicarious Liability

In Colorado, brokers can be held vicariously liable for the actions of their agents, making proper training and oversight crucial.

Disclosure of Adverse Material Facts

Colorado law requires the disclosure of adverse material facts, such as structural issues or legal impediments, to all parties.

Ethical Considerations

Code of Ethics

Many agents in Colorado are members of the National Association of Realtors (NAR), which has its own Code of Ethics that members are expected to follow.

Handling of Funds

Agents are required to handle client funds with extreme care, usually depositing them into an escrow account.

Conflict of Interest

Agents must disclose any conflict of interest, like a personal relationship with a party to the transaction, and may need to recuse themselves if the conflict is severe.

Conclusion

Understanding the laws of agency and fiduciary duties is essential for practicing real estate in Colorado. This chapter has aimed to provide a comprehensive guide to these crucial aspects of real estate law and ethics.

Action Steps for the Reader

Familiarize yourself with the different types of agency relationships and the fiduciary duties associated with each.
Understand the Colorado-specific laws and regulations that govern agency relationships.
Always act in accordance with both legal requirements and ethical standards to best serve your clients and protect yourself from liability.

By mastering the laws of agency and fiduciary duties, you'll be well-equipped to provide top-notch service to your clients and navigate the complexities of Colorado real estate law.

Mock Exam Laws of Agency and Fiduciary Duties

➡1. What is the primary role of an agent in a real estate transaction?

A. To represent the buyer only

B. To act on behalf of the principal

C. To market the property

D. To negotiate the best price for themselves

Answer: B

The primary role of an agent is to act on behalf of the principal, whether that's the buyer or the seller.

➡2. Which of the following is NOT a fiduciary duty an agent owes to their client?

A. Loyalty

B. Disclosure

C. Profit maximization

D. Confidentiality

Answer: C

Profit maximization is not a fiduciary duty. The fiduciary duties include loyalty, disclosure, and confidentiality among others.

➡3. What is dual agency?

A. When two agents represent a buyer

B. When an agent represents both buyer and seller

C. When two agents represent a seller

D. When an agent represents two buyers

Answer: B

Dual agency occurs when an agent represents both the buyer and the seller in a single transaction.

➡4. Which state law is most likely to govern real estate agency relationships?

A. Federal law

B. Common law

C. State-specific law

D. International law

Answer: C

Each state has its own set of laws and regulations governing real estate agency relationships.

➡5. What must an agent do if they are involved in a dual agency situation?

A. Keep it a secret

B. Get written consent from both parties

C. Represent the buyer's interests only

D. Represent the seller's interests only

Answer: B

In a dual agency situation, both parties must be made fully aware of the dual agency and consent to it in writing.

➡6. What does the fiduciary duty of "reasonable care and skill" entail?

A. Making the most money for the client

B. Acting as any competent agent would

C. Keeping all information confidential

D. Always being available for the client

Answer: B

The duty of "reasonable care and skill" means the agent must act as any competent agent would in the same situation.

➡7. What is the primary focus of the fiduciary duty of "loyalty"?

A. Maximizing profit for the agent

B. Putting the client's needs above the agent's

C. Keeping all information confidential

D. Disclosing all facts to the client

Answer: B

The fiduciary duty of "loyalty" requires the agent to always act in the best interest of their client.

➡8. What is the consequence of breaching fiduciary duties?

A. Loss of job

B. Legal liabilities

C. A warning

D. No consequences

Answer: B

Breaching fiduciary duties can result in various legal liabilities, including fines and loss of license.

➡9. What is the purpose of an agency agreement?

A. To outline the agent's commission

B. To outline the scope of the agent's responsibilities

C. To protect the agent from legal action

D. To list the properties for sale

Answer: B

An agency agreement outlines the scope of the agent's responsibilities and how they will be compensated.

➡10. Which of the following is **NOT** a type of agency relationship in real estate?

A. Seller's agent

B. Buyer's agent

C. Independent agent

D. Dual agent

Answer: C

"Independent agent" is not a standard type of agency relationship in real estate. The common types are seller's agent, buyer's agent, and dual agent.

➡11. What is the term for the person represented by an agent?

A. Client

B. Customer

C. Broker

D. Associate

Answer: A

The person represented by an agent is referred to as the client.

➡12. What is the fiduciary duty of "disclosure" primarily concerned with?

A. Revealing all known facts that materially affect the property

B. Keeping the client's information confidential

C. Making the most money for the client

D. Always being available for the client

Answer: A

The fiduciary duty of "disclosure" requires the agent to reveal all known facts that materially affect the property's value.

➡️**13. What is the opposite of a dual agency?**

A. Single agency

B. Triple agency

C. No agency

D. Sub-agency

Answer: A

The opposite of a dual agency is a single agency, where the agent represents only one party in the transaction.

➡️**14. What is the primary purpose of a buyer's agent?**

A. To represent the seller

B. To represent the buyer

C. To market the property

D. To negotiate the best price for themselves

Answer: B

The primary purpose of a buyer's agent is to represent the buyer's interests in the transaction.

➡️**15. What is the fiduciary duty of "obedience" concerned with?**

A. Following all of the client's lawful instructions

B. Disclosing all material facts

C. Keeping all information confidential

D. Making the most money for the client

Answer: A

The fiduciary duty of "obedience" requires the agent to follow all lawful instructions from their client.

➡16. What is the primary role of a sub-agent?

A. To represent the buyer

B. To represent the seller

C. To assist the primary agent

D. To market the property

Answer: C

The primary role of a sub-agent is to assist the primary agent in fulfilling their duties.

➡17. What is the fiduciary duty of "accounting"?

A. Keeping track of all financial transactions

B. Disclosing all material facts

C. Keeping all information confidential

D. Making the most money for the client

Answer: A

The fiduciary duty of "accounting" requires the agent to keep track of all financial transactions related to the agency relationship.

➡18. What is the primary purpose of a listing agreement?

A. To outline the buyer's needs

B. To outline the scope of the agent's responsibilities towards the seller

C. To protect the agent from legal action

D. To list the properties for rent

Answer: B

A listing agreement outlines the scope of the agent's responsibilities towards the seller and how they will be compensated.

➡**19. What is the term for an agent who represents the seller?**

A. Buyer's agent

B. Seller's agent

C. Dual agent

D. Sub-agent

Answer: B

An agent who represents the seller is known as a seller's agent.

➡**20. What is the consequence of not disclosing a dual agency?**

A. Loss of job

B. Legal liabilities

C. A warning

D. No consequences

Answer: B

Failure to disclose a dual agency can result in legal liabilities, including fines and loss of license.

➡**21. What is the primary role of a transaction broker?**

A. To represent the buyer

B. To represent the seller

C. To facilitate the transaction without representing either party

D. To market the property

Answer: C

A transaction broker's primary role is to facilitate the real estate transaction without representing either the buyer or the seller.

➡️**22. What does the fiduciary duty of "loyalty" require?**

A. Disclosing all material facts

B. Putting the client's interests above all others

C. Keeping all information confidential

D. Following all of the client's instructions

Answer: B

The fiduciary duty of "loyalty" requires the agent to put the client's interests above all others, including their own.

➡️**23. What is the term for an agent who represents both the buyer and the seller in the same transaction?**

A. Single agent

B. Dual agent

C. Sub-agent

D. Transaction broker

Answer: B

An agent who represents both the buyer and the seller in the same transaction is known as a dual agent.

➡️**24. What is the fiduciary duty of "reasonable care and diligence" concerned with?**

A. Protecting the client's financial interests

B. Disclosing all material facts

C. Keeping all information confidential

D. Following all of the client's instructions

Answer: A

The fiduciary duty of "reasonable care and diligence" requires the agent to protect the client's financial interests in the transaction.

➡️**25. What is the term for a written agreement between the agent and the client?**

A. Listing agreement

B. Agency agreement

C. Contract

D. Memorandum of understanding

Answer: B

A written agreement between the agent and the client outlining the scope of their relationship is known as an agency agreement.

➡️**26. What is the primary purpose of a seller's agent?**

A. To represent the buyer

B. To represent the seller

C. To market the property

D. To negotiate the best price for themselves

Answer: B

The primary purpose of a seller's agent is to represent the seller's interests in the transaction.

➡️**27. What is the fiduciary duty of "confidentiality" concerned with?**

A. Protecting the client's financial interests

B. Disclosing all material facts

C. Keeping all information confidential

D. Following all of the client's instructions

Answer: C

The fiduciary duty of "confidentiality" requires the agent to keep all client information confidential unless required to disclose it by law.

➡28. What is the term for an agent who does not represent either party and simply facilitates the transaction?

A. Single agent

B. Dual agent

C. Transaction broker

D. Sub-agent

Answer: C

An agent who does not represent either party and simply facilitates the transaction is known as a transaction broker.

➡29. What is the primary purpose of a dual agent?

A. To represent the buyer

B. To represent the seller

C. To represent both the buyer and the seller

D. To market the property

Answer: C

The primary purpose of a dual agent is to represent both the buyer and the seller in the same transaction.

➡30. What is the fiduciary duty of "full disclosure" concerned with?

A. Protecting the client's financial interests

B. Disclosing all material facts

C. Keeping all information confidential

D. Following all of the client's instructions

Answer: B

The fiduciary duty of "full disclosure" requires the agent to disclose all material facts that could affect the client's decisions.

➡**31. What is the term for an agent who represents the buyer exclusively?**

A. Buyer's agent

B. Seller's agent

C. Dual agent

D. Transaction broker

Answer: A

A buyer's agent exclusively represents the buyer's interests in a real estate transaction.

➡**32. What is the term used to describe the agent's responsibility to act in the best interests of the client?**

A. Loyalty

B. Obedience

C. Disclosure

D. Confidentiality

Answer: A

The term "loyalty" is used to describe the agent's fiduciary duty to act in the best interests of the client.

➡33. What is the legal obligation called when an agent must keep the client's information confidential even after the agency relationship has ended?

   A. Perpetual confidentiality

   B. Eternal secrecy

   C. Ongoing disclosure

   D. Extended loyalty

Answer: A

The legal obligation is called "perpetual confidentiality," requiring the agent to keep the client's information confidential indefinitely, even after the agency relationship has ended.

➡34. What does the fiduciary duty of "accounting" require?

   A. Keeping accurate financial records

   B. Disclosing all material facts

   C. Keeping all information confidential

   D. Following all of the client's instructions

Answer: A

The fiduciary duty of "accounting" requires the agent to keep accurate financial records related to the transaction.

➡35. What is the term for a written agreement between a buyer and an agent?

   A. Buyer's agreement

   B. Listing agreement

   C. Agency agreement

   D. Purchase agreement

Answer: A

A written agreement between a buyer and an agent is known as a buyer's agreement.

➟36. What is the primary purpose of a listing agent?

A. To represent the buyer

B. To represent the seller

C. To market the property

D. To negotiate the best price for themselves

Answer: C

The primary purpose of a listing agent is to market the property to potential buyers.

➟37. What is the fiduciary duty of "disclosure" concerned with?

A. Protecting the client's financial interests

B. Disclosing all material facts

C. Keeping all information confidential

D. Following all of the client's instructions

Answer: B

The fiduciary duty of "disclosure" requires the agent to disclose all material facts that could affect the client's decisions.

➟38. What is the term for an agent who represents the seller exclusively?

A. Buyer's agent

B. Seller's agent

C. Dual agent

D. Transaction broker

Answer: B

A seller's agent exclusively represents the seller's interests in a real estate transaction.

➡39. What is the primary role of a dual agent?

   A. To represent the buyer

   B. To represent the seller

   C. To represent both the buyer and the seller

   D. To market the property

Answer: C

The primary role of a dual agent is to represent both the buyer and the seller in the same transaction.

➡40. What is the fiduciary duty of "loyalty" concerned with?

   A. Protecting the client's financial interests

   B. Disclosing all material facts

   C. Keeping all information confidential

   D. Putting the client's interests above all others

Answer: D

The fiduciary duty of "loyalty" requires the agent to put the client's interests above all others, including their own.

➡41. What is the primary purpose of a buyer's agent in a real estate transaction?

   A. To represent the seller's interests

   B. To represent the buyer's interests

   C. To act as a neutral third party

   D. To facilitate the transaction without representation

Answer: B

The primary purpose of a buyer's agent is to represent the interests of the buyer in a real estate transaction.

➡42. What is the fiduciary duty that requires an agent to be honest and forthright with the client?

A. Loyalty

B. Disclosure

C. Obedience

D. Accountability

Answer: B

The fiduciary duty of disclosure requires an agent to be honest and forthright with the client, providing all relevant information.

➡43. What is the term for the legal relationship between a principal and an agent where the agent is expected to represent the principal's interests?

A. Contractual agreement

B. Fiduciary relationship

C. Business partnership

D. Legal guardianship

Answer: B

The term "fiduciary relationship" describes the legal relationship between a principal and an agent, where the agent is expected to represent the principal's interests with the utmost good faith, trust, confidence, and candor.

➡44. What is the fiduciary duty that requires an agent to follow all lawful instructions from the client?

A. Obedience

B. Loyalty

C. Disclosure

D. Accountability

Answer: A

The fiduciary duty of obedience requires an agent to follow all lawful instructions given by the client.

➡**45. What is the term used to describe the agent's responsibility to safeguard the client's financial interests?**

   A. Accountability

   B. Loyalty

   C. Disclosure

   D. Obedience

Answer: A

The term "accountability" is used to describe the agent's fiduciary duty to safeguard the client's financial interests.

➡**46. What is the legal obligation called when an agent must disclose any known defects of the property?**

   A. Material fact disclosure

   B. Defect revelation

   C. Condition reporting

   D. Property transparency

Answer: A

The legal obligation is called "material fact disclosure," requiring the agent to disclose any known defects of the property to the client.

➞47. What is the term used to describe the agent's responsibility to keep the client informed at all times?

A. Loyalty

B. Disclosure

C. Obedience

D. Accountability

Answer: B

The term "disclosure" is used to describe the agent's fiduciary duty to keep the client informed at all times.

➞48. In a dual agency relationship, what must the agent do to avoid conflicts of interest?

A. Represent only the buyer's interests

B. Represent only the seller's interests

C. Obtain written consent from both parties

D. Avoid disclosing any confidential information to either party

Answer: C

In a dual agency relationship, the agent must obtain written consent from both parties to avoid conflicts of interest. This ensures that both the buyer and the seller are aware of the situation and agree to it.

➞49. Which of the following is NOT a duty of an agent towards their client?

A. Confidentiality

B. Obedience

C. Disclosure

D. Independence

Answer: D

Independence is not a duty of an agent towards their client. Agents are expected to act in the best interests of their clients, which includes duties like confidentiality, obedience, and disclosure.

➡ **50. What is the term for a situation where an agent represents both the buyer and the seller in a transaction?**

  A. Double agency
  B. Single agency
  C. Sub-agency
  D. Non-agency

Answer: A

The term for a situation where an agent represents both the buyer and the seller in a transaction is called "double agency." This situation requires informed consent from both parties and can present a conflict of interest for the agent.

Property Valuation and Financial Analysis

Property valuation and financial analysis are integral aspects of real estate transactions in Colorado. Whether you're a buyer, seller, or an agent, understanding these concepts can significantly impact your decision-making process. This chapter aims to provide a comprehensive guide to property valuation methods, financial metrics, and Colorado-specific considerations.

Property Valuation Methods

Comparative Market Analysis (CMA)

CMA involves comparing the property in question to similar properties that have recently sold, are currently on the market, or were on the market but did not sell. Adjustments are made for differences like location, size, and condition.

Cost Approach

This method calculates the cost to replace the property's structure, subtracting depreciation and adding the land value. This is often used for new or specialized properties.

Income Approach

Primarily used for investment properties, this approach calculates the property's value based on its potential to generate income.

Appraisal

A formal appraisal is often required for financing and is conducted by a licensed appraiser. It may use a combination of the above methods.

Financial Analysis Metrics

Return on Investment (ROI)

ROI measures the profitability of an investment property. It is calculated by dividing the net profit by the initial investment cost.

Capitalization Rate (Cap Rate)

Cap rate is used to evaluate the potential profitability and risk of an investment property. It is calculated by dividing the property's net operating income by its current market value.

Cash Flow

Cash flow is the net income generated by the property after all expenses, including mortgage payments, maintenance, and taxes.

Loan-to-Value Ratio (LTV)

LTV is a metric used by lenders to assess the risk of a mortgage. It is calculated by dividing the loan amount by the property's appraised value.

Colorado-Specific Considerations

Seasonal Variations

Colorado's real estate market can be affected by seasonal variations, especially in tourist-heavy areas like ski resorts. This can impact both valuation and financial analysis.

Local Market Conditions

Local economic factors, such as employment rates and future development plans, can significantly affect property values.

Property Taxes

Colorado has unique property tax laws that can impact both valuation and long-term financial planning.

Water Rights

In Colorado, water rights can be a significant factor in property valuation, especially for agricultural or rural properties.

Financing Options

Conventional Loans

These are standard loans offered by banks and usually require a 20% down payment.

FHA Loans

These are government-backed loans that allow for a lower down payment but come with certain restrictions.

VA Loans

Available to veterans and active-duty military, VA loans offer benefits like no down payment and no private mortgage insurance (PMI).

Owner Financing

In some cases, the property owner may offer to finance the purchase, usually at a higher interest rate.

Risk Assessment

Market Risk

The potential for the broader real estate market to affect your property's value.

Liquidity Risk

The risk that you may not be able to sell the property quickly at market value.

Credit Risk

The risk associated with the borrower's ability to repay the loan.

Conclusion

Understanding property valuation and financial analysis is crucial for anyone involved in Colorado's real estate market. This chapter has aimed to provide a comprehensive guide to these essential aspects of real estate.

Action Steps for the Reader

1. Familiarize yourself with the various property valuation methods and financial metrics.

2. Understand the Colorado-specific factors that can impact property valuation and financial analysis.

3. Always consult with financial advisors and real estate professionals to make informed decisions.

By mastering property valuation and financial analysis, you'll be well-equipped to make informed decisions in Colorado's dynamic real estate market.

Mock Exam Property Valuation and Financial Analysis

➡1. Which property valuation method is most commonly used for residential properties?

    A. Sales Comparison Approach

    B. Cost Approach

    C. Income Approach

    D. ROI Method

Answer: A. Sales Comparison Approach

The Sales Comparison Approach is most commonly used for residential properties. It involves comparing the property to similar ones that have recently sold.

➡2. What does ROI stand for in real estate financial analysis?

    A. Return On Investment

    B. Rate Of Interest

    C. Real Estate Opportunity Index

    D. Return On Infrastructure

Answer: A. Return On Investment

ROI stands for Return On Investment. It's a key metric used to evaluate the profitability of an investment property.

➡3. What is the Debt Service Coverage Ratio (DSCR) used for?

    A. Calculating property taxes

    B. Assessing a property's ability to cover its debt obligations

    C. Determining the property's market value

    D. Calculating the monthly rent

Answer: B. Assessing a property's ability to cover its debt obligations

DSCR is used to assess a property's ability to cover its debt obligations. A DSCR greater than 1 indicates that the property is generating sufficient income to cover its debts.

➡4. Which of the following factors does NOT affect property valuation?

   A. Location

   B. Size and Layout

   C. Color of the walls

   D. Market Conditions

Answer: C. Color of the walls

The color of the walls is generally not a significant factor affecting property valuation. Location, size, and market conditions are more impactful.

➡5. What is Cash Flow Analysis used for in real estate?

   A. Calculating monthly income and expenses

   B. Assessing property taxes

   C. Determining market value

   D. Calculating ROI

Answer: A. Calculating monthly income and expenses

Cash Flow Analysis is used to calculate the monthly income generated by the property, subtracting all expenses, to determine the net cash flow.

➡6. What does a DSCR of less than 1 indicate?

   A. The property is generating sufficient income

   B. The property is not generating enough income to cover debts

   C. The property is overvalued

D. The property is undervalued

Answer: B. The property is not generating enough income to cover debts**

A DSCR of less than 1 indicates that the property is not generating sufficient income to cover its debt obligations.

➡7. In the Sales Comparison Approach, what is adjusted for when comparing properties?

A. Only the size

B. Only the location

C. Features, location, and other factors

D. Only the features

Answer: C. Features, location, and other factors

Explanation: In the Sales Comparison Approach, adjustments are made for differences in features, location, and other factors to make a fair comparison.

➡8. What is the Cost Approach commonly used for?

A. Old properties

B. New properties

C. Commercial properties

D. Rental properties

Answer: B. New properties

Explanation: The Cost Approach is often used for new properties. It involves calculating how much it would cost to replace the property, then adjusting for depreciation and land value.

➡9. Which of the following is NOT a financial analysis tool in real estate?

A. ROI

B. DSCR

C. Cash Flow Analysis

D. Gross Domestic Product (GDP)

Answer: D. Gross Domestic Product (GDP)

GDP is not a financial analysis tool used in real estate. ROI, DSCR, and Cash Flow Analysis are commonly used metrics.

➡**10. What is the Income Approach commonly used for?**

A. Residential properties

B. Commercial properties

C. New properties

D. Old properties

Answer: B. Commercial properties

The Income Approach is commonly used for commercial properties. It involves calculating the present value of future cash flows the property is expected to generate.

➡**11. What does the term 'amortization' refer to in real estate?**

A. The process of increasing property value

B. The gradual reduction of a loan balance through regular payments

C. The increase in property tax over time

D. The depreciation of property value due to age

Answer: B. The gradual reduction of a loan balance through regular payments

Amortization refers to the gradual reduction of a loan balance through regular payments over time.

➡**12. What is the primary focus of a Comparative Market Analysis (CMA)?**

A. To compare the ROI of different properties

B. To assess the fair market value of a property

C. To evaluate the debt service coverage ratio

D. To calculate the net operating income

Answer: B. To assess the fair market value of a property

A Comparative Market Analysis (CMA) is primarily used to assess the fair market value of a property by comparing it to similar properties that have recently sold or are currently on the market.

➡️**13. What does LTV stand for in real estate?**

A. Loan To Value

B. Long Term Viability

C. Lease To Vendor

D. Land Transfer Value

Answer: A. Loan To Value

LTV stands for Loan To Value, which is a ratio that compares the amount of a loan to the value of the property being purchased.

➡️**14. What is the primary purpose of a cap rate in real estate?**

A. To measure the risk associated with a property

B. To calculate the monthly mortgage payment

C. To determine the property tax rate

D. To assess the age of the property

Answer: A. To measure the risk associated with a property

The cap rate, or capitalization rate, is used to measure the risk associated with a property and its potential return on investment.

➡15. What is the formula for calculating Net Operating Income (NOI)?

   A. Gross Income - Operating Expenses

   B. Gross Income + Operating Expenses

   C. (Gross Income - Operating Expenses) / Gross Income

   D. Operating Expenses - Gross Income

Answer: A. Gross Income - Operating Expenses

Net Operating Income (NOI) is calculated by subtracting operating expenses from the gross income generated by the property.

➡16. What is the Debt Service Coverage Ratio (DSCR) primarily used for?

   A. To determine the profitability of a property

   B. To assess a borrower's ability to cover loan payments

   C. To calculate property taxes

   D. To evaluate the market value of a property

Answer: B. To assess a borrower's ability to cover loan payments

DSCR is used to evaluate a borrower's ability to cover loan payments from the property's net operating income.

➡17. What does the Gross Rent Multiplier (GRM) measure?

   A. The property's operating expenses

   B. The property's potential for appreciation

   C. The property's value relative to its gross rental income

   D. The property's maintenance costs

Answer: C. The property's value relative to its gross rental income

GRM measures the property's value in relation to its gross rental income.

➡18. What is the primary purpose of a 'due diligence' period in real estate transactions?

   A. To secure financing

   B. To conduct inspections and verify property details

   C. To negotiate the price

   D. To find tenants

Answer: B. To conduct inspections and verify property details
The due diligence period allows the buyer to conduct inspections and verify property details before finalizing the purchase.

➡19. What does the term 'equity' refer to in real estate?

   A. The market value of a property

   B. The difference between the property's market value and the outstanding loan amount

   C. The annual rental income

   D. The initial down payment

Answer: B. The difference between the property's market value and the outstanding loan amount
Equity is the difference between the market value of the property and the amount still owed on any loans.

➡20. What is a 'contingency' in a real estate contract?

   A. A binding agreement

   B. A penalty for late payment

   C. A condition that must be met for the contract to proceed

   D. An optional add-on to the contract

Answer: C. A condition that must be met for the contract to proceed

A contingency is a condition or action that must be met for a real estate contract to become binding.

→ **21. What is the primary advantage of a 'fixed-rate mortgage'?**

    A. Lower initial payments

    B. Flexibility in payment amounts

    C. Interest rate remains constant

    D. No down payment required

Answer: C. Interest rate remains constant

The main advantage of a fixed-rate mortgage is that the interest rate remains constant over the life of the loan.

→ **22. What is the 'appraisal' primarily used for in real estate?**

    A. To assess property taxes

    B. To determine the market value of a property

    C. To calculate the ROI

    D. To evaluate the property's condition

Answer: B. To determine the market value of a property

An appraisal is primarily used to determine the market value of a property, often for lending purposes.

→ **23. What does 'underwriting' refer to in the context of real estate financing?**

    A. The process of verifying loan documents

    B. The process of evaluating a borrower's creditworthiness

    C. The drafting of the mortgage contract

    D. The calculation of interest rates

Answer: B. The process of evaluating a borrower's creditworthiness
Underwriting refers to the process where a lender evaluates the creditworthiness of a potential borrower.

➡24. What is 'cash flow' in the context of real estate investment?

   A. The total value of the property
   B. The money generated after all expenses are paid
   C. The initial investment amount
   D. The annual property tax

Answer: B. The money generated after all expenses are paid
Cash flow is the money left over after all expenses, including mortgage payments and maintenance, are paid.

➡25. What does 'closing costs' include in a real estate transaction?

   A. Only the down payment
   B. Only the broker's commission
   C. Various fees like loan origination, appraisal, and legal fees
   D. Only property taxes

Answer: C. Various fees like loan origination, appraisal, and legal fees
Closing costs include a variety of fees such as loan origination fees, appraisal fees, and legal fees, among others.

➡26. What is the primary purpose of a 'cap rate' in real estate investment?

   A. To measure the risk associated with the property
   B. To calculate the property taxes
   C. To determine the mortgage interest rate
   D. To assess the property's condition

Answer: A. To measure the risk associated with the property

The cap rate is used to measure the risk and potential return of a real estate investment.

➡️**27. What does 'amortization' refer to in a mortgage context?**

A. The process of increasing property value

B. The process of paying off debt over time

C. The initial down payment

D. The annual property tax

Answer: B. The process of paying off debt over time

Amortization refers to the gradual reduction of a debt over a specified period.

➡️**28. What is a 'balloon mortgage'?**

A. A mortgage with no down payment

B. A mortgage with a large final payment

C. A mortgage with fluctuating interest rates

D. A mortgage paid off in two years

Answer: B. A mortgage with a large final payment

A balloon mortgage requires a large lump-sum payment at the end of the loan term.

➡️**29. What does 'leverage' mean in real estate investment?**

A. Using borrowed funds for investment

B. Increasing the property's value through improvements

C. The ratio of debt to equity

D. The annual rental income

Answer: A. Using borrowed funds for investment

Leverage refers to the use of borrowed funds to finance a real estate investment.

➡30. What is 'escrow' in a real estate transaction?

A. A legal agreement between buyer and seller

B. An account where funds are held until the transaction is completed

C. The commission paid to the real estate agent

D. The initial offer made by the buyer

Answer: B. An account where funds are held until the transaction is completed

Escrow is an account where funds are held by a third party until specific conditions are met.

➡31. What is the 'loan-to-value ratio' used for?

A. To determine the interest rate

B. To calculate the down payment

C. To assess the risk of the loan

D. To measure property appreciation

Answer: C. To assess the risk of the loan

The loan-to-value ratio is used by lenders to evaluate the risk associated with a mortgage loan.

➡32. What does 'negative gearing' refer to in real estate investment?

A. When rental income exceeds expenses

B. When expenses exceed rental income

C. When the property value decreases

D. When the mortgage is paid off

Answer: B. When expenses exceed rental income

Negative gearing occurs when the costs of owning a property exceed the income it generates.

➡33. What is a '1031 exchange'?

A. A tax-deferred property exchange

B. A type of mortgage

C. A property valuation method

D. A type of property insurance

Answer: A. A tax-deferred property exchange

A 1031 exchange allows the owner to sell a property and reinvest the proceeds in a new property while deferring capital gains tax.

➡34. What is 'equity' in a property?

A. The market value of the property

B. The amount owed on the mortgage

C. The property's purchase price

D. The difference between the property's value and the mortgage balance

Answer: D. The difference between the property's value and the mortgage balance

Equity is the value of ownership interest in the property, calculated as the property's market value minus the remaining mortgage balance.

➡35. What does 'due diligence' mean in a real estate context?

A. The initial deposit made by the buyer

B. The research and analysis done before purchasing a property

C. The final inspection of the property

D. The negotiation process between buyer and seller

Answer: B. The research and analysis done before purchasing a property

Due diligence refers to the comprehensive appraisal and verification of a property before buying it.

→36. What is a 'second mortgage'?

A. A mortgage taken out on a second property

B. A mortgage that replaces the first one

C. An additional loan secured by the same property

D. A mortgage with a second lender

Answer: C. An additional loan secured by the same property

A second mortgage is a loan that is secured by the equity in your home, in addition to your primary mortgage.

→37. What is 'imputed rent'?

A. Rent paid in advance

B. The rental value of a property you own and live in

C. Rent paid in installments

D. The tax on rental income

Answer: B. The rental value of a property you own and live in

Imputed rent is the economic theory of the rent you could be earning from leasing a property instead of living in it.

→38. What is a 'fixed-rate mortgage'?

A. A mortgage with fluctuating interest rates

B. A mortgage with a constant interest rate

C. A mortgage with a variable down payment

D. A mortgage that can be paid off at any time

Answer: B. A mortgage with a constant interest rate

A fixed-rate mortgage has an interest rate that remains the same for the entire term of the loan.

➟39. What is 'redlining'?

   A. A method of property valuation

   B. Discriminatory practice in lending or insurance

   C. A type of property insurance

   D. A method of calculating mortgage interest

Answer: B. Discriminatory practice in lending or insurance

Redlining is an unethical practice where services are denied or priced differently in certain areas, often based on racial or ethnic composition.

➟40. What is 'gross yield' in real estate investment?

   A. Annual rent divided by property value

   B. Monthly rent multiplied by 12

   C. Property value divided by annual rent

   D. Annual rent minus expenses

Answer: A. Annual rent divided by property value

Gross yield is calculated by taking the annual rental income, dividing it by the property value, and then multiplying by 100 to get a percentage.

➟41. What does 'amortization' refer to in a mortgage context?

   A. The process of increasing property value

   B. The process of paying off debt over time

   C. The process of calculating interest rates

   D. The process of transferring property ownership

Answer: B. The process of paying off debt over time

Amortization refers to the gradual reduction of a debt over a given period.

➡️ **42. What is a 'balloon payment'?**

A. A small initial down payment

B. A large final payment at the end of a loan term

C. A monthly mortgage payment

D. An extra payment to reduce loan principal

Answer: B. A large final payment at the end of a loan term

A balloon payment is a large, lump-sum payment made at the end of a loan's term.

➡️ **43. What is 'capital gains tax'?**

A. Tax on rental income

B. Tax on the sale of a property

C. Tax on property purchase

D. Tax on mortgage interest

Answer: B. Tax on the sale of a property

Capital gains tax is levied on the profit made from selling a property.

➡️ **44. What is a 'contingency' in a real estate contract?**

A. A penalty clause

B. A condition that must be met for the contract to proceed

C. A fixed closing date

D. A mandatory down payment

Answer: B. A condition that must be met for the contract to proceed

A contingency is a condition or action that must be met for a real estate contract to become binding.

45. What is 'escrow'?

A. A type of mortgage

B. A legal arrangement where a third party holds assets

C. A method of property valuation

D. A type of property insurance

Answer: B. A legal arrangement where a third party holds assets

Escrow is a legal concept where a financial instrument or asset is held by a third party on behalf of two other parties in a transaction.

46. What is 'net operating income' in real estate?

A. Gross income minus expenses

B. Gross income plus expenses

C. Property value minus mortgage

D. Annual rent divided by property value

Answer: A. Gross income minus expenses

Net operating income is the total income generated by a property, minus the operating expenses.

47. What does 'underwriting' refer to in real estate?

A. The process of property valuation

B. The process of assessing the risk of a loan

C. The process of property inspection

D. The process of transferring property ownership

Answer: B. The process of assessing the risk of a loan

Underwriting is the process by which a lender evaluates the risk of offering a mortgage loan.

➡48. What is 'zoning' in real estate?

A. The process of property valuation

B. The division of land into areas for specific uses

C. The process of property inspection

D. The process of transferring property ownership

Answer: B. The division of land into areas for specific uses

Zoning refers to municipal or local laws or regulations that dictate how real property can and cannot be used in certain areas.

➡49. What is 'leverage' in real estate investment?

A. Using borrowed funds for investment

B. The ratio of debt to equity

C. The process of property valuation

D. The process of property inspection

Answer: A. Using borrowed funds for investment

Leverage in real estate refers to using borrowed capital for the purpose of expanding the potential return of an investment.

➡50. What is a 'real estate bubble'?

A. A period of rapid increase in property value

B. A period of rapid decrease in property value

C. A stable real estate market

D. A period of high rental income

Answer: A. A period of rapid increase in property value

A real estate bubble refers to a period of speculative excess where property prices rise rapidly and unsustainably.

Financing

Financing is one of the most critical aspects of any real estate transaction. Whether you're a first-time homebuyer, an investor, or a seasoned real estate professional, understanding the various financing options and processes is crucial. This chapter aims to provide a comprehensive guide to financing in the context of Colorado real estate.

Types of Mortgage Loans

Fixed-Rate Mortgages

A fixed-rate mortgage has an interest rate that remains constant throughout the loan term, providing predictability in monthly payments.

Adjustable-Rate Mortgages (ARMs)

ARMs have interest rates that can change periodically, usually in relation to an index, and payments may go up or down accordingly.

Interest-Only Mortgages

These loans allow you to pay only the interest for a specific period, after which you'll start paying both principal and interest.

Balloon Mortgages

These require small monthly payments for a period, followed by a large "balloon" payment to pay off the remaining balance.

FHA Loans

Backed by the Federal Housing Administration, these loans are popular among first-time homebuyers and require a lower down payment.

VA Loans

These are available to veterans and active-duty military and offer benefits like no down payment and no private mortgage insurance (PMI).

Jumbo Loans

These are non-conforming loans that exceed the loan limits set by Fannie Mae and Freddie Mac.

Pre-Approval and Pre-Qualification

Pre-Qualification

This is an initial assessment by a lender to give you an estimate of how much you can borrow based on your income, debt, and credit history.

Pre-Approval

This is a more in-depth process where the lender checks your credit and verifies your financial and employment information to approve a specific loan amount.

Down Payments and Closing Costs

Down Payment

This is the upfront amount you pay towards the home purchase, usually ranging from 3% to 20% of the home's price.

Closing Costs

These are the additional fees and charges you'll need to pay at the time of closing, usually 2-5% of the loan amount.

Colorado-Specific Financing Options

CHFA Loans

The Colorado Housing and Finance Authority offers various loan programs to assist first-time homebuyers and those with low to moderate incomes.

Local Grants and Programs

Many Colorado counties and cities offer local grants and special financing programs to encourage homeownership.

Credit Score and Its Impact

Importance of Credit Score

Your credit score plays a significant role in determining your mortgage interest rate and eligibility.

Improving Your Credit Score

Paying off debts, keeping credit card balances low, and not opening new credit accounts can help improve your credit score.

Mortgage Insurance

Private Mortgage Insurance (PMI)

Required if your down payment is less than 20%, PMI protects the lender in case you default on the loan.

Mortgage Insurance Premium (MIP)

This is required for FHA loans, regardless of the down payment amount.

Tax Implications

Mortgage Interest Deduction

You can deduct the interest paid on your mortgage, which can offer significant tax savings.

Property Tax Deduction

Colorado allows homeowners to deduct their property taxes, which can also result in tax savings.

Conclusion

Financing is a complex but crucial aspect of real estate transactions in Colorado. This chapter has aimed to provide a comprehensive guide to help you navigate the intricacies of real estate financing.

Action Steps for the Reader

1. Understand the different types of mortgage loans and their pros and cons.
2. Get pre-qualified or pre-approved to know your borrowing capacity.
3. Explore Colorado-specific financing options that may be available to you.

By mastering the various aspects of financing, you'll be well-equipped to make informed decisions and successfully navigate Colorado's real estate market.

Mock Exam Financing

➡1. What is the minimum down payment generally required for a conventional loan?

    A. 3.5%

    B. 5%

    C. 10%

    D. 20%

Answer: **D. 20%**

Conventional loans usually require a higher down payment, often 20%, to avoid the need for mortgage insurance.

➡2. Which type of loan is backed by the Federal Housing Administration?

    A. Conventional Loan

    B. FHA Loan

    C. VA Loan

    D. ARM

Answer: **B. FHA Loan**

FHA loans are backed by the Federal Housing Administration and are designed for low-to-moderate-income borrowers.

➡3. Who is eligible for a VA loan?

    A. First-time homebuyers

    B. Veterans and active-duty military personnel

    C. Low-income borrowers

    D. Investors

Answer: B. Veterans and active-duty military personnel

VA loans are a benefit specifically for veterans and active-duty military personnel.

➠**4. What is the main feature of an Adjustable-Rate Mortgage (ARM)?**

   A. Fixed interest rate

   B. Lower initial interest rate

   C. No down payment

   D. Easier credit requirements

Answer: B. Lower initial interest rate

ARMs often start with lower rates than fixed-rate mortgages but the rates can increase over time.

➠**5. What do interest-only loans allow you to pay initially?**

   A. Only the principal

   B. Only the interest

   C. Both principal and interest

   D. Down payment only

Answer: B. Only the interest

Interest-only loans allow you to pay just the interest for a specific initial period, usually 5-10 years.

➠**6. What is the first step in the mortgage process?**

   A. Loan Application

   B. Pre-Approval

   C. Underwriting

   D. Closing

Answer: B. Pre-Approval

Before looking at properties, it's advisable to get pre-approved for a mortgage, which involves a lender checking your financial background.

➡7. **What does the underwriting process involve?**

    A. Property inspection

    B. Financial due diligence

    C. Property selection

    D. Loan repayment

Answer: B. Financial due diligence

During underwriting, the lender assesses your financial situation in detail and checks the property appraisal.

➡8. **What is usually included in closing costs?**

    A. Monthly mortgage payments

    B. Down payment

    C. Loan origination fees

    D. Property taxes

Answer: C. Loan origination fees

Closing costs can include loan origination fees, appraisal fees, title searches, and more.

➡9. **What can significantly impact your monthly mortgage payments?**

    A. Type of property

    B. Real estate agent's commission

    C. Interest rates

    D. Home inspection fees

Answer: C. Interest rates

The interest rate on your mortgage will significantly impact your monthly payments and the overall cost of the loan.

➠10. What is often included in monthly mortgage payments and paid by the lender annually?

    A. Closing costs

    B. Down payment

    C. Property taxes and homeowner's insurance

    D. Mortgage insurance

Answer: C. Property taxes and homeowner's insurance

Property taxes and homeowner's insurance are often included in monthly mortgage payments and are then paid by the lender on an annual basis.

➠11. What is the purpose of a good faith estimate?

    A. To provide an estimate of closing costs

    B. To lock in an interest rate

    C. To guarantee loan approval

    D. To assess property value

    Answer: A. To provide an estimate of closing costs

    A good faith estimate is provided by the lender to give you an idea of your closing costs.

➠12. What is a balloon mortgage?

    A. A mortgage with fluctuating interest rates

    B. A mortgage that requires a large payment at the end

    C. A mortgage with no down payment

    D. A mortgage with very low monthly payments

Answer: B. A mortgage that requires a large payment at the end

A balloon mortgage requires a large lump sum payment at the end of the loan term.

➡️13. What does LTV stand for?

A. Loan To Value

B. Long Term Viability

C. Loan Transfer Variable

D. Low Transaction Volume

Answer: A. Loan To Value

LTV stands for Loan To Value, which is the ratio of the loan amount to the value of the property.

➡️14. What is a home equity loan?

A. A loan for first-time homebuyers

B. A loan based on the value of your home

C. A loan for home repairs

D. A loan for investment properties

Answer: B. A loan based on the value of your home

A home equity loan is a type of loan where the borrower uses the equity of their home as collateral.

➡️15. What is PMI?

A. Property Management Insurance

B. Private Mortgage Insurance

C. Public Mortgage Index

D. Property Maintenance Inclusion

Answer: B. Private Mortgage Insurance

PMI stands for Private Mortgage Insurance, which is usually required when the down payment is less than 20%.

➡**16. What is a reverse mortgage?**

    A. A mortgage for seniors to convert equity into cash

    B. A mortgage with reverse interest rates

    C. A mortgage that pays the borrower

    D. A mortgage for investment properties

Answer: A. A mortgage for seniors to convert equity into cash

A reverse mortgage allows seniors to convert the equity in their home into cash, usually for living expenses.

➡**17. What is the main advantage of a 15-year mortgage over a 30-year mortgage?**

    A. Lower interest rates

    B. Lower monthly payments

    C. No down payment

    D. No closing costs

Answer: A. Lower interest rates

A 15-year mortgage typically offers lower interest rates and allows you to build equity faster.

➡**18. What does refinancing a mortgage mean?**

    A. Changing the terms of your mortgage

    B. Extending your mortgage term

    C. Taking out a second mortgage

    D. Defaulting on your mortgage

Answer: A. Changing the terms of your mortgage

Refinancing involves replacing your existing mortgage with a new one, usually with better terms.

➡ **19. What is a credit score primarily used for in the mortgage process?**

    A. To determine eligibility for certain types of loans

    B. To decide the size of the down payment

    C. To set the property value

    D. To calculate closing costs

Answer: A. To determine eligibility for certain types of loans

Your credit score is used to determine your eligibility for loans and the interest rate you'll receive.

➡ **20. What is a jumbo loan?**

    A. A loan for small properties

    B. A loan exceeding conforming loan limits

    C. A loan for commercial properties

    D. A loan for mobile homes

Answer: B. A loan exceeding conforming loan limits

A jumbo loan is a mortgage that exceeds the conforming loan limits set by federal agencies.

➡ **21. What is the primary purpose of an escrow account in a mortgage?**

    A. To hold the down payment

    B. To pay property taxes and insurance

    C. To cover repair costs

    D. To pay off the mortgage early

Answer: B. To pay property taxes and insurance

An escrow account is typically used to hold funds for paying property taxes and insurance.

➡22. What is an adjustable-rate mortgage (ARM)?

    A. A mortgage with a fixed interest rate

    B. A mortgage with an interest rate that can change

    C. A mortgage with no interest

    D. A mortgage for investment properties

Answer: B. A mortgage with an interest rate that can change

An adjustable-rate mortgage has an interest rate that can change periodically depending on market conditions.

➡23. What is the debt-to-income ratio?

    A. The ratio of your monthly debt payments to your monthly income

    B. The ratio of your loan amount to your property value

    C. The ratio of your credit score to your income

    D. The ratio of your down payment to your loan amount

Answer: A. The ratio of your monthly debt payments to your monthly income

The debt-to-income ratio is used by lenders to assess your ability to manage payments.

➡24. What is a pre-qualification in the mortgage process?

    A. A binding agreement between you and the lender

    B. An estimate of how much you can borrow

    C. A guarantee of a loan

    D. A final approval for a loan

Answer: B. An estimate of how much you can borrow

Pre-qualification is an initial step that gives you an estimate of how much you may be able to borrow.

➡️**25. What is the main disadvantage of an interest-only mortgage?**

    A. You can't pay off the principal
    B. You pay more interest over time
    C. You can't refinance
    D. You need a large down payment

Answer: B. You pay more interest over time
With an interest-only mortgage, you end up paying more in interest because you're not reducing the principal.

➡️**26. What does APR stand for?**

    A. Annual Property Rate
    B. Annual Percentage Rate
    C. Approved Payment Rate
    D. Average Price Range

Answer: B. Annual Percentage Rate
APR stands for Annual Percentage Rate, which includes the interest rate and other loan costs.

➡️**27. What is a conforming loan?**

    A. A loan that meets federal guidelines
    B. A loan for investment properties
    C. A loan with no down payment
    D. A loan with a variable interest rate

Answer: A. A loan that meets federal guidelines

A conforming loan is one that adheres to the guidelines set by Fannie Mae and Freddie Mac.

➡ **28. What is a VA loan?**

    A. A loan for veterans

    B. A loan for vacation homes

    C. A loan for very large properties

    D. A loan for agricultural properties

Answer: A. A loan for veterans

A VA loan is a mortgage loan in the United States guaranteed by the United States Department of Veterans Affairs.

➡ **29. What is the main advantage of a fixed-rate mortgage?**

    A. Lower interest rates

    B. Interest rate can decrease

    C. Monthly payments stay the same

    D. No down payment required

Answer: C. Monthly payments stay the same

With a fixed-rate mortgage, your monthly payments are predictable because the interest rate stays the same.

➡ **30. What is underwriting in the context of mortgages?**

    A. The process of verifying financial information

    B. The process of selling a mortgage

    C. The process of setting interest rates

    D. The process of inspecting a property

Answer: A. The process of verifying financial information

Underwriting involves verifying your financial information and assessing the risk of offering you a loan.

➡31. What is a balloon payment?

    A. A small monthly payment

    B. A large final payment

    C. A payment made annually

    D. A payment made bi-weekly

Answer: B. A large final payment

A balloon payment is a large, lump-sum payment made at the end of a loan term.

➡32. What is the purpose of private mortgage insurance (PMI)?

    A. To protect the borrower from foreclosure

    B. To protect the lender if the borrower defaults

    C. To lower the interest rate

    D. To eliminate the need for a down payment

Answer: B. To protect the lender if the borrower defaults

PMI is designed to protect the lender in case the borrower defaults on the loan.

➡33. What is the primary purpose of an amortization schedule?

    A. To show the breakdown of each monthly payment into principal and interest

    B. To show the total amount of interest paid over the life of the loan

    C. To show the property's appreciation value over time

    D. To show the borrower's credit score

Answer: A. To show the breakdown of each monthly payment into principal and interest

An amortization schedule provides a detailed breakdown of each monthly payment, showing how much goes toward the principal and how much goes toward interest.

➡34. What is a fixed-rate mortgage?

    A. A mortgage with an interest rate that changes over time

    B. A mortgage with a constant interest rate for the life of the loan

    C. A mortgage with varying monthly payments

    D. A mortgage with no interest

Answer: B. A mortgage with a constant interest rate for the life of the loan
A fixed-rate mortgage has an interest rate that remains the same for the entire term of the loan, providing predictability in payments.

➡35. What is a home equity line of credit (HELOC)?

    A. A fixed-rate loan

    B. A revolving line of credit

    C. A type of insurance

    D. A government grant

Answer: B. A revolving line of credit
A HELOC is a revolving line of credit that uses your home as collateral.

➡36. What is the loan-to-value ratio (LTV)?

    A. The ratio of the loan amount to the property value

    B. The ratio of the down payment to the loan amount

    C. The ratio of the interest rate to the loan amount

    D. The ratio of the loan amount to the borrower's income

Answer: A. The ratio of the loan amount to the property value

The loan-to-value ratio is the amount of the loan compared to the value of the property.

→ **37. What is a subprime mortgage?**

    A. A mortgage for borrowers with excellent credit

    B. A mortgage for borrowers with poor credit

    C. A mortgage with no interest

    D. A mortgage for commercial properties

Answer: B. A mortgage for borrowers with poor credit

A subprime mortgage is designed for borrowers who have poor credit history.

→ **38. What is refinancing?**

    A. Taking out a second mortgage

    B. Replacing an existing loan with a new one

    C. Changing the terms of your existing loan

    D. Selling your mortgage to another lender

Answer: B. Replacing an existing loan with a new one

Refinancing involves replacing an existing loan with a new one, usually with better terms.

→ **39. What is a bridge loan?**

    A. A loan for construction projects

    B. A short-term loan to cover the period between two long-term loans

    C. A loan for first-time homebuyers

    D. A loan for renovating a property

Answer: B. A short-term loan to cover the period between two long-term loans

A bridge loan is a short-term loan used until a person secures permanent financing.

⇢40. What is a seller carry-back?

    A. When the seller pays the closing costs

    B. When the seller acts as the lender

    C. When the seller pays for repairs

    D. When the seller pays the agent's commission

Answer: B. When the seller acts as the lender

In a seller carry-back, the seller provides financing to the buyer, essentially acting as the lender.

⇢41. What is the Loan-to-Value (LTV) ratio?

    A. The ratio of the loan amount to the property's appraised value

    B. The ratio of the loan amount to the borrower's income

    C. The ratio of the property's appraised value to the market value

    D. The ratio of the down payment to the loan amount

Answer: A. The ratio of the loan amount to the property's appraised value

The Loan-to-Value (LTV) ratio is calculated by dividing the loan amount by the property's appraised value.

⇢42. What does a balloon payment refer to?

    A. A large final payment at the end of a loan term

    B. Monthly payments that gradually decrease

    C. An initial down payment

    D. Monthly payments that gradually increase

Answer: A. A large final payment at the end of a loan term

A balloon payment is a large, lump-sum payment made at the end of a loan's term.

➡43. What is the purpose of a "good faith estimate" in mortgage lending?

    A. To provide an estimate of closing costs

    B. To lock in an interest rate

    C. To assess the borrower's creditworthiness

    D. To determine the property's market value

Answer: A. To provide an estimate of closing costs

A "good faith estimate" is provided by the lender to give the borrower an estimate of the closing costs involved in the mortgage process.

➡44. What does the term "amortization" refer to in the context of a mortgage?

    A. The process of increasing the loan amount

    B. The process of paying off the loan over time

    C. The process of adjusting the interest rate

    D. The process of transferring the loan to another lender

Answer: B. The process of paying off the loan over time.

Amortization refers to the process of gradually paying off a loan over a specified period, usually through regular payments that cover both principal and interest.

➡45. What is the primary advantage of a fixed-rate mortgage over an adjustable-rate mortgage?

    A. Lower initial interest rate

    B. Interest rate can decrease over time

    C. Interest rate remains constant over the loan term

    D. Easier qualification criteria

    Answer: C. Interest rate remains constant over the loan term

The primary advantage of a fixed-rate mortgage is that the interest rate remains constant over the term of the loan, providing predictability in payments.

➡ 46. What is private mortgage insurance (PMI)?

A. Insurance that protects the lender

B. Insurance that protects the borrower

C. Insurance that protects the property

D. Insurance that protects against natural disasters

Answer: A. Insurance that protects the lender

PMI is insurance that protects the lender in case the borrower defaults on the loan.

➡ 47. What is an escrow account primarily used for?

A. Investing in stocks

B. Paying property taxes and insurance

C. Saving for retirement

D. Paying off the mortgage early

Answer: B. Paying property taxes and insurance

An escrow account is typically used to pay property taxes and insurance premiums.

➡ 48. What is a debt-to-income ratio?

A. The ratio of a borrower's total debt to total income

B. The ratio of a borrower's credit score to income

C. The ratio of a borrower's assets to liabilities

D. The ratio of a borrower's monthly expenses to income

Answer: A. The ratio of a borrower's total debt to total income

The debt-to-income ratio is calculated by dividing a borrower's total debt by their total income.

➡ 49. What is the primary purpose of a rate lock?

    A. To increase the interest rate over time

    B. To decrease the interest rate over time

    C. To secure an interest rate for a specified period

    D. To allow the interest rate to fluctuate

Answer: C. To secure an interest rate for a specified period

A rate lock secures a specific interest rate for a set period, usually during the loan application process.

➡ 50. What is a pre-qualification?

    A. A binding agreement between the lender and borrower

    B. An initial assessment of a borrower's creditworthiness

    C. A final approval for a loan

    D. A legal document outlining the terms of the loan

Answer: B. An initial assessment of a borrower's creditworthiness

A pre-qualification is an initial evaluation of a borrower's creditworthiness, usually based on self-reported financial information.

Transfer of Property

The transfer of property is a pivotal moment in any real estate transaction. It's the point where ownership changes hands, and various legal and financial processes come into play. This chapter aims to provide a comprehensive guide to the transfer of property in Colorado, covering everything from the initial contract to the final recording of the deed.

The Sales Contract

Elements of a Valid Contract

A valid sales contract in Colorado must include an offer, acceptance, consideration, and the legal capacity of both parties to enter into the contract.

Contingencies

Contingencies are conditions that must be met for the contract to proceed. Common contingencies include financing approval, successful home inspection, and clear title.

Earnest Money

This is a deposit made by the buyer to show good faith. In Colorado, earnest money is usually held in an escrow account until closing.

Title Search and Insurance

Title Search

A title search is conducted to ensure that the seller has a clear title to the property, free from liens or other encumbrances.

Title Insurance

This protects the buyer and lender against any future claims to the property. In Colorado, it's customary for the seller to pay for the owner's title insurance, while the buyer pays for the lender's title insurance.

The Closing Process

Pre-Closing Steps

Before closing, the buyer should conduct a final walk-through, and both parties should review the closing disclosure form, which outlines the final financial details.

The Closing Table

At closing, the buyer and seller, along with their agents and attorneys, meet to finalize the transaction. Documents are signed, and funds are exchanged.

Recording the Deed

After closing, the deed is recorded in the county where the property is located, officially transferring ownership to the buyer.

Colorado-Specific Regulations

Disclosure Requirements

Colorado law requires sellers to disclose any material defects in the property, usually through a Seller's Property Disclosure form.

Water Rights

In Colorado, water rights can be a significant factor in property transfers, especially for rural or agricultural properties.

Transfer Taxes

Colorado has a documentary fee based on the sales price of the property, usually paid by the buyer.

Common Issues and How to Avoid Them

Clouded Title

A clouded title can delay or even cancel a property transfer. Always conduct a thorough title search to avoid this.

Financing Delays

Ensure that all financing is in place well before the closing date to avoid delays.

Property Condition

Disputes over the property's condition can derail a transaction. Always conduct thorough inspections and negotiate repairs beforehand.

Conclusion

The transfer of property in Colorado involves multiple steps, each with its own set of regulations and potential pitfalls. This chapter has aimed to provide a comprehensive guide to help you navigate this complex process.

Action Steps for the Reader

1. Familiarize yourself with the elements of a valid sales contract and common contingencies.

2. Understand the importance of a title search and title insurance.

3. Be prepared for the closing process and be aware of Colorado-specific regulations that may apply.

By mastering the process of property transfer, you'll be well-equipped to navigate the complexities of Colorado real estate transactions.

Mock Exam Transfer of Property

➠1. What is the most common form of voluntary property transfer?

   A. Foreclosure

   B. Eminent Domain

   C. Sales

   D. Adverse Possession

Answer: C. Sales

Sales are the most common form of voluntary property transfer, usually involving a straightforward transaction between a buyer and a seller.

➠2. Which type of deed offers the least protection to the buyer?

   A. General Warranty Deed

   B. Special Warranty Deed

   C. Quitclaim Deed

   D. Bargain and Sale Deed

Answer: C. Quitclaim Deed

Quitclaim Deeds offer the least protection as they come with no warranties.

➠3. What is the legal process by which a lender can take possession of a property due to default?

   A. Eminent Domain

   B. Foreclosure

   C. Adverse Possession

   D. Gifting

Answer: B. Foreclosure

Foreclosure is the legal process that allows a lender to take possession of a property when the owner defaults on mortgage payments.

➡4. What is the minimum requirement for a deed to be enforceable?

A. Oral Agreement

B. Written Instrument

C. Mutual Consent

D. Legal Capacity

Answer: B. Written Instrument

A deed must be in writing to be legally enforceable, complying with state laws.

➡5. What does a Preliminary Title Report outline?

A. Tax implications of the sale

B. Issues with the title

C. Financing options

D. Property valuation

Answer: B. Issues with the title

A Preliminary Title Report outlines any issues with the title that need to be resolved before the sale can proceed.

➡6. What is the purpose of opening an escrow account?

A. To hold funds and documents related to the transaction

B. To pay property taxes

C. To hold the seller's profit

D. To pay the real estate agent's commission

Answer: A. To hold funds and documents related to the transaction

An escrow account is opened to securely hold funds and documents related to the property transaction until all conditions are met.

➡7. What is the term for gaining ownership of a property by occupying it for an extended period under certain conditions?

   A. Eminent Domain
   B. Foreclosure
   C. Adverse Possession
   D. Inheritance

Answer: C. Adverse Possession

Adverse Possession allows someone to gain ownership of a property by occupying it for an extended period, provided certain legal conditions are met.

➡8. What type of deed only covers the period of the current owner's tenure?

   A. General Warranty Deed
   B. Special Warranty Deed
   C. Quitclaim Deed
   D. Bargain and Sale Deed

Answer: B. Special Warranty Deed

A Special Warranty Deed only covers the period of the current owner's tenure and does not extend back to the property's origins.

➡9. What is the term for the government acquiring private property for public use?

   A. Foreclosure
   B. Eminent Domain
   C. Adverse Possession

D. Gifting

Answer: B. Eminent Domain

Eminent Domain is the legal process by which the government can acquire private property for public use, provided they offer just compensation.

➡10. What is the most common form of consideration in property transfers?

A. Services

B. Money

C. Other assets

D. Promissory notes

Answer: B. Money

Money is the most common form of consideration in property transfers, although other assets or services can also serve this purpose.

➡11. What is the term for a legal claim against a property that must be paid off when the property is sold?

A. Lien

B. Mortgage

C. Easement

D. Covenant

Answer: A. Lien

A lien is a legal claim against a property that must be paid off when the property is sold.

➡12. What is the right to use someone else's land for a specific purpose called?

A. Easement

B. Lien

C. Covenant

D. Mortgage

Answer: A. Easement

An easement grants the right to use another person's land for a specific purpose.

➟13. What is the process of dividing a large parcel of land into smaller lots?

A. Zoning

B. Subdivision

C. Partitioning

D. Rezoning

Answer: B. Subdivision

Subdivision is the process of dividing a larger parcel of land into smaller lots.

➟14. What is the term for a restriction on how a property may be used?

A. Easement

B. Covenant

C. Lien

D. Mortgage

Answer: B. Covenant

A covenant is a restriction on how a property may be used, often found in property deeds or community bylaws.

➟15. What is the primary purpose of a title search?

A. To determine property value

B. To find any restrictions on the property

C. To discover any liens or encumbrances on the property

D. To assess the property's condition

Answer: C. To discover any liens or encumbrances on the property

The primary purpose of a title search is to discover any liens, encumbrances, or other issues that could affect the transfer of property.

➡️**16. What is the term for the transfer of property upon the owner's death without a will?**

A. Probate
B. Intestate
C. Testamentary
D. Inheritance

Answer: B. Intestate

When a property owner dies without a will, the property is transferred according to intestate laws.

➡️**17. What is the term for a change in property ownership where the new owner assumes the mortgage?**

A. Assumption
B. Novation
C. Subletting
D. Foreclosure

Answer: A. Assumption

Assumption is when a new owner takes over the existing mortgage of the property.

➡️**18. What is the term for the right of a government or its agent to expropriate private property for public use, with payment of compensation?**

A. Eminent Domain

B. Foreclosure

C. Adverse Possession

D. Lien

Answer: A. Eminent Domain

Eminent Domain is the right of a government to expropriate private property for public use, with compensation.

➡**19. What is the term for a written document that transfers title of property from one person to another?**

A. Mortgage

B. Deed

C. Lien

D. Easement

Answer: B. Deed

A deed is a written document that transfers title of property from one person to another.

➡**20. What is the term for a legal process that involves the distribution of a deceased person's property?**

A. Probate

B. Intestate

C. Foreclosure

D. Eminent Domain

Answer: A. Probate

Probate is the legal process involving the distribution of a deceased person's property, especially if they died without a will.

➡21. What is the term for acquiring property through the unauthorized occupation of another's land?

A. Adverse Possession

B. Eminent Domain

C. Foreclosure

D. Probate

Answer: A. Adverse Possession

Adverse Possession is the process of acquiring property by occupying someone else's land without permission for a certain period of time.

➡22. What is the term for a legal document that confirms the sale of a property?

A. Bill of Sale

B. Deed of Trust

C. Title Certificate

D. Warranty Deed

Answer: A. Bill of Sale

A Bill of Sale is a legal document that confirms the sale and transfer of property from one party to another.

➡23. What is the term for a legal claim by a lender on the title of a property until a debt is paid off?

A. Mortgage

B. Lien

C. Easement

D. Covenant

Answer: A. Mortgage

A mortgage is a legal claim by a lender on the title of a property until the debt secured by the mortgage is paid off.

➡24. What is the term for the legal process by which a lender takes possession of a property due to non-payment?

   A. Foreclosure

   B. Eminent Domain

   C. Probate

   D. Adverse Possession

Answer: A. Foreclosure

Foreclosure is the legal process by which a lender takes possession of a property due to the borrower's failure to make required payments.

➡25. What is the term for a legal agreement that allows one party to use another's property for a specific purpose?

   A. Lease

   B. Mortgage

   C. Easement

   D. Lien

Answer: A. Lease

A lease is a legal agreement that allows one party to use another's property for a specific period and for a specific purpose.

➡26. What is the term for the official document that records the ownership of a property?

A. Title Certificate

B. Bill of Sale

C. Deed of Trust

D. Warranty Deed

Answer: A. Title Certificate

A Title Certificate is the official document that records the ownership of a property.

➡ **27. What is the term for a legal restriction on the use of land?**

A. Zoning

B. Easement

C. Mortgage

D. Lien

Answer: A. Zoning

Zoning is a legal restriction that dictates how land in a certain area can be used.

➡ **28. What is the term for the right of a property owner to use and enjoy their property without interference?**

A. Quiet Enjoyment

B. Eminent Domain

C. Probate

D. Foreclosure

Answer: A. Quiet Enjoyment

Quiet Enjoyment is the right of a property owner to use and enjoy their property without interference from others.

➡29. What is the term for a legal document that outlines the terms under which a loan will be repaid?

   A. Promissory Note
   B. Bill of Sale
   C. Title Certificate
   D. Warranty Deed

Answer: A. Promissory Note

A Promissory Note is a legal document that outlines the terms under which a loan will be repaid.

➡30. What is the term for the legal process of transferring property from a deceased person to their heirs?

   A. Inheritance
   B. Probate
   C. Foreclosure
   D. Eminent Domain

Answer: B. Probate

Probate is the legal process of transferring property from a deceased person to their heirs, especially if there is no will.

➡31. What is the term for the legal process that allows the government to take private property for public use?

   A. Eminent Domain
   B. Foreclosure
   C. Adverse Possession
   D. Probate

Answer: A. Eminent Domain

Eminent Domain is the legal process that allows the government to take private property for public use, usually with compensation to the owner.

➡**32. What is the term for a legal agreement that secures a loan with real property?**

A. Deed of Trust

B. Bill of Sale

C. Lease

D. Promissory Note

Answer: A. Deed of Trust

A Deed of Trust is a legal agreement that secures a loan with real property and serves as protection for the lender.

➡**33. What is the term for the legal right to use a portion of another person's property for a specific purpose, such as a driveway or pathway?**

A. Easement

B. Lien

C. Covenant

D. Right of Way

Answer: A. Easement

An easement is the legal right to use a portion of another person's property for a specific purpose, such as a driveway or pathway.

➡**34. What is the term for a legal document that transfers ownership of property from the seller to the buyer?**

A. Warranty Deed

B. Bill of Sale

C. Title Certificate

D. Promissory Note

Answer: A. Warranty Deed

A Warranty Deed is a legal document that transfers ownership of property from the seller to the buyer.

➞**35.** What is the term for the legal right to pass through someone else's land?

A. Right of Way

B. Easement

C. Zoning

D. Lien

Answer: A. Right of Way

Right of Way is the legal right to pass through someone else's land, often established through an easement.

➞**36.** What is the term for a legal document that outlines the terms of a rental agreement?

A. Lease Agreement

B. Bill of Sale

C. Deed of Trust

D. Promissory Note

Answer: A. Lease Agreement

A Lease Agreement is a legal document that outlines the terms of a rental agreement between a landlord and tenant.

➞**37.** What is the term for the legal process of verifying the validity of a will?

A. Probate

B. Eminent Domain

C. Foreclosure

D. Adverse Possession

Answer: A. Probate

Probate is the legal process of verifying the validity of a will and distributing the deceased's assets according to the will.

➡**38. What is the term for a legal restriction placed on a property by a previous owner?**

A. Covenant

B. Easement

C. Lien

D. Zoning

Answer: A. Covenant

A covenant is a legal restriction placed on a property by a previous owner, often outlined in the deed.

➡**39. What is the term for the legal process of dividing a large parcel of land into smaller lots?**

A. Subdivision

B. Zoning

C. Easement

D. Lien

Answer: A. Subdivision

Subdivision is the legal process of dividing a large parcel of land into smaller lots, often for the purpose of development.

➡️40. What is the term for a legal document that grants someone the right to act on behalf of another in legal matters?

    A. Power of Attorney

    B. Lease Agreement

    C. Deed of Trust

    D. Promissory Note

Answer: A. Power of Attorney

Power of Attorney is a legal document that grants someone the right to act on behalf of another in legal matters.

➡️41. What is the primary purpose of a deed restriction?

    A. To limit the use of the property

    B. To transfer ownership

    C. To secure a loan

    D. To establish easements

Answer: A. To limit the use of the property

Deed restrictions are used to limit the use of the property according to the terms set by the owner or the community.

➡️42. What is the difference between a general warranty deed and a quitclaim deed?

    A. A general warranty deed provides no warranties

    B. A quitclaim deed provides full warranties

    C. A general warranty deed provides full warranties

    D. Both provide the same level of warranties

Answer: C. A general warranty deed provides full warranties

A general warranty deed provides the most protection to the buyer as it includes full warranties against any encumbrances.

➡ **43. What is the role of a title company in a property transaction?**

A. Financing the purchase

B. Ensuring the title is clear

C. Conducting home inspections

D. Setting the property's price

Answer: B. Ensuring the title is clear

The title company ensures that the title to a piece of real estate is legitimate and then issues title insurance for that property.

➡ **44. What is the term for a written summary of a property's ownership history?**

A. Title report

B. Chain of title

C. Deed of trust

D. Abstract of title

Answer: D. Abstract of title

An abstract of title is a written summary of a property's ownership history, which is used to determine the current status of the title.

➡ **45. What is the purpose of a gift deed?**

A. To transfer property as a gift

B. To secure a mortgage

C. To lease the property

D. To sell the property

Answer: A. To transfer property as a gift

A gift deed is used to transfer property ownership without any exchange of money.

➡46. What is a defeasible fee estate?

A. An estate that can be defeated or terminated

B. An estate that lasts forever

C. An estate that is free from encumbrances

D. An estate that is leased

Answer: A. An estate that can be defeated or terminated

A defeasible fee estate is a type of estate that can be defeated or terminated upon the occurrence of a specific event.

➡47. What is the primary purpose of a deed?

A. To prove ownership of personal property

B. To transfer ownership of real property

C. To outline the terms of a mortgage

D. To establish a rental agreement

Answer: B. To transfer ownership of real property

The primary purpose of a deed is to transfer ownership of real property from one party to another. It serves as a legal document that shows the change in ownership.

➡48. What is the primary purpose of a land contract?

A. To lease land

B. To sell land

C. To gift land

D. To mortgage land

Answer: B. To sell land

A land contract is primarily used to sell land, where the seller provides financing to the buyer.

➡️49. What is the term for the right of the government to take private property for public use?

A. Eminent domain

B. Escheat

C. Foreclosure

D. Adverse possession

Answer: A. Eminent domain

Eminent domain is the right of the government to take private property for public use, with compensation to the owner.

➡️50. What is the process of dividing a single property into smaller parcels?

A. Zoning

B. Subdivision

C. Partition

D. Condemnation

Answer: B. Subdivision

Subdivision is the process of dividing a single property into smaller parcels, often for the purpose of development.

Practice of Real Estate and Disclosures

The practice of real estate in Colorado involves a myriad of responsibilities, from ethical considerations to legal obligations. One of the most critical aspects is the disclosure of information. This chapter aims to provide a comprehensive guide on the practice of real estate and the importance of disclosures in Colorado.

Licensing and Regulation

Real Estate Commission

The Colorado Real Estate Commission oversees the licensing and regulation of real estate professionals in the state.

Licensing Requirements

To become a licensed real estate agent in Colorado, you must complete pre-licensing education, pass the state exam, and meet other criteria like background checks.

Continuing Education

Colorado requires real estate professionals to complete continuing education courses to maintain their licenses.

Ethical Practices

Code of Ethics

The National Association of Realtors (NAR) has a Code of Ethics that all Realtors are expected to follow.

Fiduciary Duties

Real estate agents have fiduciary duties to their clients, including loyalty, confidentiality, and full disclosure.

Fair Housing Laws

Colorado adheres to federal Fair Housing Laws, which prohibit discrimination based on race, color, religion, sex, or national origin.

Disclosures in Colorado

Seller's Property Disclosure

Colorado law requires sellers to provide a Seller's Property Disclosure form, detailing the condition of the property.

Lead-Based Paint Disclosure

For homes built before 1978, federal law requires a lead-based paint disclosure.

Square Footage Disclosure

Colorado requires the disclosure of the property's square footage, but it's often advisable to verify this independently.

Water Rights Disclosure

In Colorado, water rights can be a significant factor, especially for rural properties. These must be disclosed in the sales contract.

Contracts and Agreements

Listing Agreement

This is a contract between the seller and the real estate agent, outlining the terms of the property's sale.

Buyer's Agency Agreement

This agreement outlines the responsibilities of the agent towards the buyer, including fiduciary duties and the scope of work.

Purchase Agreement

This is the main contract in a real estate transaction, outlining the terms and conditions of the sale.

Technology in Real Estate Practice

MLS Systems

Multiple Listing Service (MLS) systems are widely used in Colorado for listing properties and conducting market analysis.

Virtual Tours

Virtual tours have become increasingly popular, especially during the COVID-19 pandemic, as a way to showcase properties.

Digital Signatures

Colorado allows the use of digital signatures in real estate transactions, making the process more efficient.

Conclusion

The practice of real estate in Colorado is governed by a complex set of laws, regulations, and ethical guidelines. Disclosures play a crucial role in ensuring transparency and trust between all parties involved.

Action Steps for the Reader

1. If you're an aspiring real estate professional, familiarize yourself with Colorado's licensing requirements and ethical guidelines.
2. If you're a buyer or seller, be aware of your rights and responsibilities, especially concerning disclosures.
3. Always consult with professionals, such as real estate agents and attorneys, to guide you through the complexities of real estate practice in Colorado.

By understanding the practice of real estate and the importance of disclosures, you'll be better equipped to navigate the Colorado real estate market successfully.

Mock Exam Practice of Real Estate and Disclosures

➡1. What is the primary focus of residential sales in real estate practice?

   A. Lease agreements

   B. Market trends

   C. Zoning laws

   D. Property management

Answer: **B**

Residential sales primarily focus on understanding market trends, property values, and the needs of clients.

➡2. What does a property manager NOT typically handle?

   A. Rent collection

   B. Maintenance and repairs

   C. Property appraisals

   D. Tenant relations

Answer: **C**

Property managers usually do not handle property appraisals; that's the job of a certified appraiser.

➡3. What is a material fact in real estate disclosures?

   A. The color of the walls

   B. The age of the roof

   C. The seller's reason for moving

   D. The brand of appliances in the home

Answer: B

Material facts include significant issues like the age of the roof, which could affect the property's value and condition.

➞4. What is the primary role of a leasing agent?

A. Property valuation

B. Finding tenants

C. Handling legal actions

D. Managing day-to-day operations

Answer: B

Leasing agents focus on finding tenants for vacant properties.

➞5. What must be disclosed about homes built before 1978?

A. Asbestos

B. Radon

C. Lead-based paint

D. All of the above

Answer: C

Federal law requires the disclosure of lead-based paint for homes built before 1978.

➞6. Who is responsible for providing a Seller's Property Disclosure?

A. Buyer

B. Seller

C. Real estate agent

D. Home inspector

Answer: B

The seller is responsible for filling out the Seller's Property Disclosure form.

➡7. What is NOT a type of disclosure in real estate?

A. Seller's Property Disclosure

B. Agency Disclosures

C. Financial Disclosures

D. Buyer's Property Disclosure

Answer: D

There is no such thing as a Buyer's Property Disclosure; the seller provides all necessary disclosures.

➡8. What does a real estate appraiser provide?

A. Legal advice

B. Estimated property value

C. Lease agreements

D. Tenant screening

Answer: B

Real estate appraisers provide an estimated value of a property.

➡9. What is included in natural hazards disclosures?

A. Property age

B. Utility availability

C. Flood risk

D. Previous owners

Answer: C

Natural hazards disclosures may include information on flood risk, earthquakes, and other natural disasters.

➥10. What is the primary ethical obligation of a real estate professional?

A. Maximizing profit

B. Acting in the best interests of their clients

C. Avoiding legal repercussions

D. Networking

Answer: B

Real estate professionals are ethically bound to act in the best interests of their clients.

➥11. What is the primary purpose of a Comparative Market Analysis (CMA)?

A. To determine property taxes

B. To set a listing price

C. To assess zoning laws

D. To evaluate mortgage options

Answer: B

A Comparative Market Analysis is primarily used to set a listing price for a property based on similar properties in the area.

➥12. What does the acronym RESPA stand for?

A. Real Estate Settlement Procedures Act

B. Residential Estate Sales Professional Association

C. Real Estate Service Providers Act

D. Residential Environmental Safety Protocol Act

Answer: A

RESPA stands for Real Estate Settlement Procedures Act, which regulates closing costs and settlement procedures.

➡️13. What is the role of a fiduciary in real estate?

A. To provide financing

B. To act in the best interest of the client

C. To appraise the property

D. To market the property

Answer: B

A fiduciary is obligated to act in the best interest of the client.

➡️14. What is NOT a common type of real estate fraud?

A. Property flipping

B. Equity skimming

C. False advertising

D. Open listing

Answer: D

Open listing is a type of listing agreement, not a form of real estate fraud.

➡️15. What is the main purpose of a title search?

A. To find the property's market value

B. To verify the legal owner of the property

C. To assess the property's condition

D. To determine the property's zoning status

Answer: B

The main purpose of a title search is to verify the legal owner of the property.

➡16. What is a latent defect?

    A. A defect that is visible during a walk-through

    B. A defect that is hidden and not easily discoverable

    C. A defect that has been repaired

    D. A defect listed in the property disclosure

Answer: B

A latent defect is a hidden defect that is not easily discoverable during a routine inspection.

➡17. What is the primary purpose of a home inspection?

    A. To assess the property's market value

    B. To identify any defects or issues with the property

    C. To verify the property's legal status

    D. To finalize the mortgage terms

Answer: B

The primary purpose of a home inspection is to identify any defects or issues with the property.

➡18. What is a short sale?

    A. A quick sale process

    B. Selling the property for less than the mortgage owed

    C. A sale with few contingencies

    D. A sale where the buyer pays in cash

Answer: B

A short sale is when the property is sold for less than the amount owed on the mortgage.

➠19. What is earnest money?

    A. The commission for the real estate agent

    B. A deposit made by the buyer

    C. The final payment at closing

    D. Money paid for a home inspection

Answer: B

Earnest money is a deposit made by the buyer to show their serious intent to purchase the property.

➠20. What does a contingency in a real estate contract allow?

    A. Immediate possession of the property

    B. The buyer to back out under specific conditions

    C. The seller to change the listing price

    D. The real estate agent to collect a higher commission

Answer: B

A contingency allows the buyer to back out of the purchase under specific conditions without losing their earnest money.

➠21. What is the primary role of the Multiple Listing Service (MLS)?

    A. To provide mortgage rates

    B. To list properties for sale

    C. To regulate real estate agents

    D. To assess property taxes

Answer: B

The primary role of the MLS is to list properties for sale, making it easier for agents to find properties for their clients.

→22. What is a dual agency?

A. When two agents represent the buyer

B. When one agent represents both the buyer and the seller

C. When two agents represent the seller

D. When an agent represents two buyers in the same transaction

Answer: B

Dual agency occurs when one agent represents both the buyer and the seller in a real estate transaction.

→23. What is the main purpose of a seller's disclosure?

A. To list the price of the property

B. To disclose any known defects or issues with the property

C. To describe the property's features

D. To outline the commission rates

Answer: B

The main purpose of a seller's disclosure is to disclose any known defects or issues with the property.

→24. What does the term "underwater mortgage" mean?

A. A mortgage with a high interest rate

B. A mortgage that is higher than the property's value

C. A mortgage for a property near a body of water

D. A mortgage that has been paid off

Answer: B

An underwater mortgage is when the remaining mortgage balance is higher than the current market value of the property.

25. What is a "pocket listing"?

A. A listing that is not yet on the market

B. A listing that is only shared with a select group of agents

C. A listing that has been sold

D. A listing that is under contract

Answer: B

A pocket listing is a listing that is not publicly advertised and is only shared with a select group of agents.

26. What is the main purpose of a buyer's agent?

A. To list properties for sale

B. To represent the buyer's interests

C. To conduct home inspections

D. To provide financing options

Answer: B

The main purpose of a buyer's agent is to represent the interests of the buyer in a real estate transaction.

27. What is a "balloon payment"?

A. A small monthly payment

B. A large final payment at the end of a mortgage term

C. A payment made halfway through the mortgage term

D. A payment made to the real estate agent

Answer: B

A balloon payment is a large final payment due at the end of a mortgage term.

28. What is "redlining"?

A. Drawing property boundaries

B. Discriminatory practice in lending or insurance

C. Highlighting important clauses in a contract

D. Marking properties that are under contract

Answer: B

Redlining is a discriminatory practice where services like lending or insurance are denied or priced higher for residents of certain areas.

29. What is the main purpose of an escrow account?

A. To hold the earnest money deposit

B. To pay the real estate agent's commission

C. To store the property's title

D. To hold funds for property taxes and insurance

Answer: D

The main purpose of an escrow account is to hold funds for property taxes and insurance.

30. What is a "contingent offer"?

A. An offer that is higher than the listing price

B. An offer that is dependent on certain conditions being met

C. An offer that has been accepted but not yet closed

D. An offer that is non-negotiable

Answer: B

A contingent offer is an offer that is dependent on certain conditions being met, such as financing or a satisfactory home inspection.

➡31. What is the primary role of a "listing agent"?

A. To represent the buyer in a transaction

B. To represent the seller in a transaction

C. To conduct the home inspection

D. To provide financing options

Answer: B

The primary role of a listing agent is to represent the seller in a real estate transaction, helping them to sell their property.

➡32. What is a "short sale"?

A. A quick sale of a property

B. Selling a property for less than the mortgage owed

C. Selling a property without an agent

D. A discounted sale for a quick closing

Answer: B

A short sale is when a property is sold for less than the amount owed on the mortgage.

➡33. What is "title insurance"?

A. Insurance for property damage

B. Insurance that protects against defects in the title

C. Insurance for the mortgage lender

D. Insurance for the real estate agent

Answer: B

Title insurance protects against defects in the title to the property.

➡34. What is "earnest money"?

A. Money paid to the real estate agent

B. Money paid to secure a contract

C. Money paid for a home inspection

D. Money paid for closing costs

Answer: B

Earnest money is a deposit made to a seller to show the buyer's good faith in a transaction.

➡ 35. What is a "FSBO" listing?

A. For Sale By Owner

B. For Sale By Operator

C. For Sale Before Offer

D. For Sale By Order

Answer: A

FSBO stands for "For Sale By Owner," indicating that the property is being sold without a real estate agent.

➡ 36. What is "amortization"?

A. The process of increasing property value

B. The process of paying off a loan over time

C. The process of transferring property

D. The process of evaluating a property's worth

Answer: B

Amortization is the process of paying off a loan over time through regular payments.

➡ 37. What is a "home warranty"?

A. A guarantee on the home's structure

B. A guarantee on the home's appliances and systems

C. A guarantee on the home's value

D. A guarantee on the home's location

Answer: B

A home warranty is a service contract that covers the repair or replacement of important home system components and appliances.

→**38. What is "zoning"?**

A. The process of measuring a property

B. The division of land into areas for specific uses

C. The process of evaluating a property's value

D. The process of transferring property

Answer: B

Zoning is the division of land into areas designated for specific uses, such as residential, commercial, or industrial.

→**39. What is a "pre-approval letter"?**

A. A letter confirming the property's value

B. A letter confirming mortgage eligibility

C. A letter confirming the property's condition

D. A letter confirming the real estate agent's credentials

Answer: B

A pre-approval letter is a letter from a lender indicating that a buyer is eligible for a mortgage up to a certain amount.

→**40. What is "escrow"?**

A. A type of mortgage

B. A legal arrangement where a third party holds assets

C. A type of home inspection

D. A type of real estate contract

Answer: B

Escrow is a legal arrangement in which a third party holds assets on behalf of the buyer and seller.

→41. What is the purpose of a "Seller's Disclosure Statement"?

A. To disclose the seller's financial status

B. To disclose any known defects or issues with the property

C. To disclose the commission rate of the real estate agents

D. To disclose the buyer's financing options

Answer: B

The Seller's Disclosure Statement is used to disclose any known defects or issues with the property to potential buyers.

→42. What does "dual agency" mean in real estate?

A. Two agents working for the same brokerage

B. An agent representing both the buyer and the seller

C. Two buyers competing for the same property

D. Two lenders involved in the financing

Answer: B

Dual agency occurs when a real estate agent represents both the buyer and the seller in the same transaction.

➡43. What is the primary purpose of a "title search"?

A. To find the property's market value

B. To check for any liens or encumbrances on the property

C. To assess the property's condition

D. To determine the zoning laws affecting the property

Answer: B

The primary purpose of a title search is to check for any liens or encumbrances on the property.

➡44. What does "FSBO" stand for?

A. For Sale By Owner

B. Full Service Brokerage Option

C. Fixed Selling Bonus Offer

D. Final Sale Before Offer

Answer: A

FSBO stands for "For Sale By Owner," indicating that the property is being sold directly by the owner without the representation of a real estate agent.

➡45. What is a "contingency" in a real estate contract?

A. A mandatory clause

B. A binding agreement

C. A condition that must be met for the contract to proceed

D. A non-negotiable term

Answer: C

A contingency is a condition that must be met for the contract to proceed.

➡46. What is the role of an "escrow agent"?

A. To market the property

B. To hold and disburse funds during a transaction

C. To negotiate the contract terms

D. To inspect the property

Answer: B

The role of an escrow agent is to hold and disburse funds during a real estate transaction.

➡47. What does "amortization" refer to?

A. The process of increasing property value

B. The process of paying off a loan over time

C. The process of transferring property ownership

D. The process of evaluating a property's worth

Answer: B

Amortization refers to the process of paying off a loan over time through regular payments.

➡48. What is the "right of first refusal" in a real estate context?

A. The right to refuse a home inspection

B. The right to be the first to make an offer on a property

C. The right to refuse to pay closing costs

D. The right to refuse to honor a contract

Answer: B

The right of first refusal gives a person the opportunity to be the first to make an offer on a property before the owner sells it to someone else.

➡49. What does "encumbrance" refer to in real estate?

A. A type of insurance policy

B. A claim or lien on a property

C. A type of mortgage loan

D. A legal restriction on property use

Answer: B

An encumbrance is a claim or lien on a property that affects its use or transfer.

➡50. What does "under contract" mean in real estate?

A. The property is being appraised

B. The property is available for sale

C. The property has an accepted offer but has not yet closed

D. The property is off the market

Answer: C

"Under contract" means that the property has an accepted offer but the sale has not yet closed.

Contracts

Contracts are the backbone of any real estate transaction. They define the terms, conditions, and obligations of all parties involved. This chapter aims to provide a comprehensive guide on the various types of contracts you'll encounter in Colorado real estate and how to navigate them effectively.

Types of Real Estate Contracts

Listing Agreement

This is a contract between a seller and a real estate agent, outlining the terms under which the property will be marketed and sold.

Buyer's Agency Agreement

This agreement establishes the relationship between the buyer and the real estate agent, specifying the agent's responsibilities and compensation.

Purchase Agreement

Also known as a sales contract, this document outlines the terms and conditions of the property sale, including price, contingencies, and closing date.

Lease Agreement

For rental properties, a lease agreement defines the terms under which a tenant can use and occupy the property.

Land Contract

This is a seller-financed agreement where the buyer makes payments directly to the seller until the full purchase price is paid.

Essential Elements of a Contract

Offer and Acceptance

A contract begins with an offer from one party and acceptance by another. Both must be clear and unequivocal.

Consideration

This is something of value exchanged between parties, often the property and the money.

Legal Capacity

Both parties must have the legal capacity to enter into a contract, meaning they are of sound mind and not under any form of duress.

Legality of Purpose

The contract must be for a legal purpose. Any contract based on illegal activities is void.

Contingencies in Contracts

Financing Contingency

This allows the buyer to back out if they are unable to secure financing.

Inspection Contingency

This gives the buyer the right to have the property inspected and to renegotiate or withdraw if issues are found.

Appraisal Contingency

This protects the buyer if the property is appraised for less than the purchase price.

Title Contingency

This allows the buyer to withdraw if a clear title cannot be provided.

Colorado-Specific Contract Provisions

Earnest Money

In Colorado, earnest money is often required to show the buyer's serious intent.

Water Rights

Given the importance of water in Colorado, water rights are often a key contract provision.

Property Taxes

Colorado contracts often specify how property taxes will be prorated between the buyer and seller.

HOA Regulations

If the property is part of a Homeowners Association, the contract should specify any related fees or rules.

Contract Breaches and Remedies

Types of Breaches

A breach occurs when one party fails to fulfill their contractual obligations.

Remedies

Remedies can include monetary damages, specific performance, or contract termination.

Conclusion

Contracts in Colorado real estate are complex but crucial. They define the rules of engagement for all parties and provide legal remedies if things go awry.

Action Steps for the Reader

1. Familiarize yourself with the types of contracts you'll encounter in Colorado real estate.

2. Understand the essential elements that make a contract legally binding.

3. Be aware of common contingencies and how they can affect your transaction.

By mastering the intricacies of real estate contracts, you'll be well-equipped to navigate the complexities of the Colorado real estate market.

Mock Exam Contracts

➡1. What is the primary purpose of a Purchase Agreement in real estate?

A. To outline the commission for the real estate agent

B. To set the stage for the relationship between buyer and seller

C. To provide a warranty for the property

D. To list the property on MLS

Answer: B

The Purchase Agreement serves as the cornerstone of any real estate transaction, outlining the terms and conditions between the buyer and seller.

➡2. Which type of lease requires the tenant to pay a flat rent while the landlord pays for all property charges?

A. Gross Lease

B. Net Lease

C. Triple Net Lease

D. Modified Gross Lease

Answer: A

In a Gross Lease, the tenant pays a flat rent and the landlord is responsible for all property charges.

➡3. What is "Consideration" in a contract?

A. A thoughtful gesture

B. Money or something of value exchanged

C. A legal requirement

D. A counteroffer

Answer: B

Consideration refers to something of value that is exchanged between parties in a contract. It can be money, services, or even a promise.

➡4. What happens in a Material Breach of contract?

A. A minor failure in performance

B. A significant failure in performance

C. A legal dispute

D. Contract is automatically renewed

Answer: B

A Material Breach is a significant failure in performance that allows the other party to seek remedies.

➡5. Which clause in a contract specifies what will happen if issues are found during an inspection?

A. Contingency Clause

B. Disclosure Clause

C. Inspection Clause

D. Arbitration Clause

Answer: C

The Inspection Clause outlines the type of inspection, who will conduct it, and what actions will be taken if issues are found.

➡6. What does a "Straight Option" in an Option Agreement provide?

A. The right to lease the property

B. The exclusive right to purchase within a certain time

C. The right to sublease the property

D. The right to first refusal

Answer: B

A Straight Option gives the buyer the exclusive right to purchase the property within a specified time frame.

➡7. Who cannot legally enter into a contract?

A. A licensed real estate agent

B. A minor

C. A property manager

D. A real estate investor

Answer: B

Minors are not legally competent to enter into contracts.

➡8. What is the primary purpose of Disclosure Clauses?

A. To outline the commission structure

B. To state federal and state requirements for property disclosure

C. To specify the type of inspection

D. To set the rent amount in a lease

Answer: B

Disclosure Clauses are used to state federal and state requirements for property disclosure, such as the presence of lead paint.

➡9. What is a Conditional Sale Agreement?

A. The property is sold as-is

B. The sale is conditional upon certain criteria

C. The buyer has the option to purchase later

D. The seller can back out at any time

Answer: B

A Conditional Sale Agreement means the sale is conditional upon certain criteria being met, such as the sale of the buyer's current home.

➡10. What is the legal status of a contract for illegal activities?

A. Valid

B. Null and void

C. Conditional

D. Binding

Answer: B

Contracts for illegal activities are considered null and void.

➡11. What is the role of an "Escrow Agent" in a real estate contract?

A. To market the property

B. To hold and disburse funds

C. To conduct inspections

D. To negotiate terms

Answer: B

The Escrow Agent holds and disburses funds according to the terms of the contract.

➡12. Which of the following is NOT a required element for a contract to be valid?

A. Offer and acceptance

B. Consideration

C. Legal purpose

D. Notarization

Answer: D

Notarization is not a required element for a contract to be valid.

➡13. **What is the "Statute of Frauds" in relation to contracts?**

A. A law that makes oral contracts illegal

B. A law that requires certain contracts to be in writing

C. A law that prevents fraudulent activities

D. A law that nullifies all previous contracts

Answer: B

The Statute of Frauds requires certain contracts, like those for real estate, to be in writing to be enforceable.

➡14. **What does "Time is of the Essence" mean in a contract?**

A. The contract has no expiration date

B. The contract must be executed within a specific timeframe

C. The contract can be modified at any time

D. The contract is not urgent

Answer: B

"Time is of the Essence" means that the contract must be executed within a specific timeframe, and delays could lead to penalties or termination of the contract.

➡15. **What is a "Right of First Refusal"?**

A. The right to reject any offer

B. The right to match or better any offer received by the seller

C. The right to be the first to view a property

D. The right to terminate a contract without penalty

Answer: B

The Right of First Refusal allows the holder to match or better any offer received by the seller before the property is sold to another party.

➡16. What is a "Contingent Contract"?

A. A contract that is dependent on certain conditions being met

B. A contract that is legally binding

C. A contract that has been terminated

D. A contract that is in the negotiation phase

Answer: A

A Contingent Contract is dependent on certain conditions being met, such as financing approval or a satisfactory home inspection.

➡17. What is "Specific Performance"?

A. A clause that specifies the responsibilities of each party

B. A legal remedy for breach of contract

C. A type of contract used in commercial real estate

D. A measure of a real estate agent's effectiveness

Answer: B

Specific Performance is a legal remedy that forces the breaching party to fulfill the terms of the contract.

➡18. What is the purpose of a "Hold Harmless Clause"?

A. To protect the buyer from market fluctuations

B. To protect one or both parties from liability for the actions of the other

C. To hold the property off the market for a specific period

D. To hold the buyer's deposit in escrow

Answer: B

A Hold Harmless Clause protects one or both parties from liability for the actions or negligence of the other party.

➡19. What is a "Bilateral Contract"?

A. A contract where only one party is obligated to perform

B. A contract where both parties are obligated to perform

C. A contract that is null and void

D. A contract that has been terminated

Answer: B

In a Bilateral Contract, both parties are obligated to perform their respective duties.

➡20. What is the "Implied Covenant of Good Faith and Fair Dealing"?

A. A written clause in every contract

B. An unwritten obligation for parties to act honestly and not cheat each other

C. A legal doctrine that makes all contracts public

D. A requirement for all contracts to be reviewed by a lawyer

Answer: B

The Implied Covenant of Good Faith and Fair Dealing is an unwritten obligation that requires parties to act honestly and not cheat or mislead each other.

➡21. What is a "Unilateral Contract"?

A. A contract where only one party is obligated to perform

B. A contract where both parties are obligated to perform

C. A contract that is null and void

D. A contract that has been terminated

Answer: A

In a Unilateral Contract, only one party is obligated to perform, while the other has the option but not the obligation to perform.

➡ 22. What is "Liquidated Damages"?

A. The actual damages suffered due to a breach

B. A pre-determined amount to be paid in case of a breach

C. The refundable part of a deposit

D. The non-refundable part of a deposit

Answer: B

Liquidated Damages are a pre-determined amount agreed upon by the parties to be paid in case of a breach of contract.

➡ 23. What is "Novation"?

A. The act of renewing a contract

B. The act of replacing one party in a contract with another

C. The act of nullifying a contract

D. The act of negotiating the terms of a contract

Answer: B

Novation is the act of replacing one party in a contract with another, effectively transferring the obligations to the new party.

➡ 24. What is an "Addendum"?

A. A change to the original contract

B. A separate agreement that is included with the original contract

C. A summary of the contract

D. A legal interpretation of the contract

Answer: B

An Addendum is a separate agreement that is included with the original contract to add or clarify terms.

➡25. What is "Recission"?

A. The act of renewing a contract

B. The act of terminating a contract and restoring parties to their original positions

C. The act of transferring a contract

D. The act of amending a contract

Answer: B

Recission is the act of terminating a contract and restoring the parties to their original positions, as if the contract had never existed.

➡26. What is "Parol Evidence"?

A. Written evidence

B. Oral evidence

C. Photographic evidence

D. Video evidence

Answer: B

Parol Evidence refers to oral statements or agreements that are not included in the written contract.

➡27. What is a "Counteroffer"?

A. An acceptance of the original offer

B. A rejection of the original offer

C. A new offer made in response to an original offer

D. A legal requirement for all contracts

Answer: C

A Counteroffer is a new offer made in response to an original offer, effectively rejecting the original offer.

➡️**28. What is "Earnest Money"?**

A. Money paid to confirm a contract

B. Money paid to a real estate agent

C. Money held in escrow

D. Money paid for a home inspection

Answer: A

Earnest Money is money paid to confirm a contract, showing the buyer's serious intent to purchase.

➡️**29. What is "Force Majeure"?**

A. A clause that frees both parties from liability in case of an extraordinary event

B. A clause that holds both parties liable regardless of circumstances

C. A clause that allows for price negotiation

D. A clause that requires a third-party mediator

Answer: A

Force Majeure is a clause that frees both parties from liability in case of an extraordinary event, like a natural disaster, that prevents one or both parties from fulfilling the contract.

➡️**30. What is "Severability"?**

A. The ability to separate a contract into individual clauses

B. The ability to terminate a contract without penalty

C. The ability to transfer a contract to another party

D. The ability to amend a contract after signing

Answer: A

Severability is the ability to separate a contract into individual clauses, so that if one clause is found to be unenforceable, the rest of the contract remains in effect.

➡31. What does "Statute of Frauds" require for a real estate contract to be enforceable?

A. Verbal agreement

B. Written and signed agreement

C. Notarized agreement

D. Witnessed agreement

Answer: B

The Statute of Frauds requires that a real estate contract must be in writing and signed by the parties to be enforceable.

➡32. What is "Specific Performance"?

A. Monetary compensation for breach of contract

B. Forcing a party to carry out the terms of the contract

C. Nullifying the contract

D. Amending the contract

Answer: B

Specific Performance is a legal remedy that forces a party to carry out the terms of the contract as agreed.

➡33. What is "Time is of the Essence" in a contract?

A. A clause that allows for flexible deadlines

B. A clause that makes deadlines strictly binding

C. A clause that nullifies the contract after a certain time

D. A clause that allows for automatic renewal of the contract

Answer: B

"Time is of the Essence" is a clause that makes deadlines strictly binding, and failure to meet them could lead to breach of contract.

➡34. What is an "Open Listing"?

A. A listing agreement with multiple brokers

B. A listing agreement with one broker

C. A listing that is not publicly advertised

D. A listing that is only advertised within a brokerage

Answer: A

An Open Listing is a listing agreement where the seller can employ multiple brokers who can bring buyers to the property.

➡35. What is a "Net Listing"?

A. A listing where the broker's commission is a percentage of the sale price

B. A listing where the broker keeps all amounts above a certain price

C. A listing where the broker charges a flat fee

D. A listing where the broker's commission is paid by the buyer

Answer: B

In a Net Listing, the broker agrees to sell the owner's property for a set price, and anything above that price is kept as the broker's commission.

➡36. What is a "Contingency" in a contract?

A. A fixed term

B. A condition that must be met for the contract to be binding

C. A penalty for breach of contract

D. An optional term

Answer: B

A Contingency is a condition that must be met for the contract to proceed to closing.

➡ 37. What is "Due Diligence" in the context of a real estate contract?

A. The buyer's investigation of the property

B. The seller's disclosure of property defects

C. The broker's marketing efforts

D. The lender's appraisal of the property

Answer: A

Due Diligence refers to the buyer's investigation of the property to discover any issues that were not disclosed.

➡ 38. What is "Escrow"?

A. A legal process to resolve disputes

B. A third-party account where funds are held until conditions are met

C. A type of mortgage

D. A tax levied on property sales

Answer: B

Escrow is a third-party account where funds or assets are held until contractual conditions are met.

➡ 39. What is "Right of First Refusal"?

A. The right to be the first to purchase a property

B. The right to refuse any offer on a property

C. The right to terminate a contract

D. The right to amend a contract

Answer: A

Right of First Refusal gives a person the opportunity to be the first to purchase a property before the owner sells it to someone else.

→40. What is "Joint Tenancy"?

A. Ownership by one individual

B. Ownership by two or more individuals with equal shares

C. Ownership by a corporation

D. Ownership by tenants

Answer: B

Joint Tenancy is a form of ownership where two or more individuals own property with equal shares and have the right of survivorship.

→41. What is the primary purpose of a "Letter of Intent" in a real estate transaction?

A. To serve as a binding contract

B. To outline the terms under which a contract will be negotiated

C. To legally transfer property

D. To terminate an existing contract

Answer: B

A Letter of Intent serves to outline the terms under which the parties will negotiate a contract. It is generally not binding.

→42. What does "Time is of the Essence" mean in a real estate contract?

A. The contract has an indefinite period

B. The contract must be executed within a specific timeframe

C. The contract can be terminated at any time

D. The contract is not time-sensitive

Answer: B

"Time is of the Essence" means that the contract must be executed within a specific timeframe, and failure to do so could result in penalties or termination of the contract.

→43. What is the purpose of an "Addendum" in a real estate contract?

A. To correct a typo or error

B. To add additional terms or conditions

C. To terminate the contract

D. To renew the contract

Answer: B

An Addendum is used to add additional terms or conditions to an existing contract, effectively modifying it.

→44. What is the effect of a "Waiver" in a contract?

A. It adds a new term to the contract

B. It removes a party's right to enforce a term of the contract

C. It extends the contract's duration

D. It makes the contract voidable

Answer: B

A waiver removes a party's right to enforce a particular term of the contract, essentially giving up that right.

➡️45. What is "Specific Performance" in the context of a real estate contract?

A. Monetary compensation

B. Carrying out the exact terms of the contract

C. Termination of the contract

D. An optional performance

Answer: B

Specific Performance refers to carrying out the exact terms of the contract, usually enforced through a court order.

➡️46. What does "Novation" mean in a contract?

A. Renewal of the contract

B. Replacement of one party with another

C. Addition of a new term

D. Termination of the contract

Answer: B

Novation means the replacement of one party in the contract with another, effectively transferring the obligations to the new party.

➡️47. What does "Force Majeure" refer to in a contract?

A. A type of fraud

B. An act of God or unforeseen circumstances

C. A breach of contract

D. A type of contingency

Answer: B

Force Majeure refers to unforeseen circumstances or "acts of God" that prevent one or both parties from fulfilling the contract. It usually allows for the contract to be terminated or suspended.

➡48. What is the role of an "Escrow Agent"?

A. To negotiate the contract
B. To hold and disburse funds or documents
C. To enforce the contract
D. To terminate the contract

Answer: B

An Escrow Agent holds and disburses funds or documents as per the terms of the contract.

➡49. What is "Right of First Refusal" in a real estate contract?

A. The right to back out of the contract first
B. The right to match any offer received by the seller
C. The right to inspect the property first
D. The right to make the first offer on a property

Answer: B

Right of First Refusal gives a party the right to match any offer received by the seller, usually before the property is sold to another buyer.

➡50. What is "Earnest Money" in the context of a real estate contract?

A. The commission for the real estate agent
B. A deposit made by the buyer to show good faith
C. The final payment made at closing
D. A refundable deposit

Answer: B

Earnest Money is a deposit made by the buyer to show good faith and secure the contract.

It is usually non-refundable and is applied to the purchase price.

Real Estate Calculations

Real estate calculations are an integral part of the real estate industry. Whether you're an agent, a buyer, or an investor, understanding the numbers is crucial. This chapter will delve into the most important calculations you'll encounter, from mortgage payments to investment returns.

Property Valuation

- Comparative Market Analysis (CMA)

A Comparative Market Analysis (CMA) is the cornerstone of property valuation. It involves comparing the property in question to similar properties ("comparables" or "comps") that have recently sold in the area.

Formula:

Property Value = Average Price of Comparable Properties x (1 + Adjustment Factor)}

Why It Matters:

Understanding how to accurately perform a CMA can mean the difference between overpricing a property, causing it to sit on the market, or underpricing it and losing money.

- Capitalization Rate

The capitalization rate, or cap rate, is another essential metric for property valuation, particularly for income-generating properties.

Formula:

$$\text{Cap Rate} = \frac{Net\ Operating\ Income}{Current\ Market\ Value}$$

Why It Matters:

The cap rate gives you a quick way to compare the profitability of different investment properties.

Financing Calculations

- Mortgage Payments

Mortgage calculations are essential for both buyers and real estate professionals to understand.

Formula:

$$M = P \times \frac{r(1+r)^n}{(1+r)^n - 1}$$

Where :

M is the monthly payment,

P is the principal loan amount,

r is the monthly interest rate, and

n is the number of payments.

Why It Matters:

Knowing how to calculate mortgage payments allows you to assess the affordability of a property and helps in planning long-term finances.

- Loan-to-Value Ratio (LTV)

The Loan-to-Value ratio is a risk assessment metric that lenders use.

Formula:

$$LTV = \frac{Loan\ Amount}{Appraised\ Value} \times 100$$

Why It Matters:

A high LTV ratio might mean a riskier loan from a lender's perspective, potentially requiring the borrower to purchase mortgage insurance.

Investment Calculations

- Return on Investment (ROI)

ROI is a measure of the profitability of an investment.

Formula:

$$\text{ROI} = \frac{Net\ Profit}{Cost\ of\ Investment} \times 100$$

Why It Matters:

ROI gives you a snapshot of the investment's performance, helping you compare it against other investment opportunities.

- Cash-on-Cash Return

This metric gives you the annual return on your investment based on the cash flow and the amount of money you've invested.

Formula:

$$\text{Cash-on-Cash Return} = \frac{Annual\ Cash\ Flow}{Total\ Cash\ Invested} \times 100$$

Why It Matters:

Cash-on-cash return is crucial for understanding the cash income you're generating compared to the cash invested, providing a more accurate picture of an investment's performance.

Area and Volume Calculations

- Square Footage

Square footage is the measure of an area, and it's one of the most basic calculations in real estate.

Formula:

Area = Length x Width

Why It Matters:

Square footage affects everything from listing prices to renovation costs, so getting it right is crucial.

- Cubic Footage

Cubic footage is often used in commercial real estate to determine the volume of a space.

Formula:

Volume = Length x Width x Height

Why It Matters:

In commercial settings, cubic footage can be essential for understanding how a space can be used.

Prorations and Commissions

- Prorations

Prorations are used to divide property taxes, insurance premiums, or other costs between the buyer and seller.

Formula:

$$\text{Proration Amount} = \frac{\textit{Annual Cost}}{365} \times \textbf{Number of Days}$$

Why It Matters:

Prorations ensure that both parties are only paying for their share of the costs during the time they own the property.

- Commission Calculation

Commissions are the lifeblood of most real estate agents and brokers.

Formula:

Commission = Sale Price x Commission Rate

Why It Matters:

Understanding how commissions are calculated can help agents set realistic business goals and expectations.

Conclusion

Mastering these calculations is not just a requirement for passing various real estate exams; it's a necessity for a successful career in real estate. This chapter has covered the essential calculations any real estate professional needs to understand.

Mock Exam Real Estate Calculations

→1. What is the formula for calculating the Loan-to-Value ratio?

A. Loan Amount / Appraised Value

B. Appraised Value / Loan Amount

C. Loan Amount × Appraised Value

D. Appraised Value × Loan Amount

Answer: A

The Loan-to-Value ratio is calculated as Loan Amount divided by Appraised Value.

→2. What does ROI stand for?

A. Return On Investment

B. Rate Of Interest

C. Real Estate Opportunity

D. Rate Of Inflation

Answer: A

ROI stands for Return On Investment, which measures the profitability of an investment.

→3. What is the formula for calculating square footage?

A. Length × Width

B. Length × Height

C. Length + Width

D. Length / Width

Answer: A

Square footage is calculated by multiplying the length by the width of the area.

➡4. What is the formula for calculating mortgage payments?

A. P × (r(1+r)^n) / ((1+r)^n-1)

B. P × r × n

C. P / r × n

D. P × n / r

Answer: A

The formula for calculating mortgage payments is **P × (r(1+r)^n) / ((1+r)^n-1)**.

➡5. What is the formula for calculating the capitalization rate?

A. Net Operating Income / Current Market Value

B. Current Market Value / Net Operating Income

C. Net Operating Income × Current Market Value

D. Current Market Value × Net Operating Income

Answer: A

The capitalization rate is calculated as **Net Operating Income divided by Current Market Value.**

➡6. What does CMA stand for in real estate calculations?

A. Comparative Market Analysis

B. Capital Market Assessment

C. Current Market Appraisal

D. Comparative Monetary Assessment

Answer: A

CMA stands for Comparative Market Analysis, used for property valuation.

➡7. What is the formula for calculating Cash-on-Cash Return?

A. Annual Cash Flow / Total Cash Invested × 100

B. Total Cash Invested / Annual Cash Flow × 100

C. Annual Cash Flow × Total Cash Invested

D. Total Cash Invested × Annual Cash Flow

Answer: A

Cash-on-Cash Return is calculated as Annual Cash Flow divided by Total Cash Invested, multiplied by 100.

➡8. What is the formula for calculating prorations?

A. Annual Cost / 365 × Number of Days

B. Annual Cost × 365 / Number of Days

C. Number of Days / Annual Cost × 365

D. Number of Days × Annual Cost / 365

Answer: A

Prorations are calculated as Annual Cost divided by 365, multiplied by the Number of Days.

➡9. What is the formula for calculating cubic footage?

A. Length × Width × Height

B. Length × Width

C. Length × Height

D. Width × Height

Answer: A

Cubic footage is calculated by multiplying the length, width, and height of the space.

➡10. What is the formula for calculating commissions?

A. Sale Price × Commission Rate

B. Commission Rate × Sale Price

C. Sale Price / Commission Rate

D. Commission Rate / Sale Price

Answer: A

Commissions are calculated as Sale Price multiplied by Commission Rate.

➡**11. What is the formula for calculating Gross Rent Multiplier (GRM)?**

A. Property Price / Gross Annual Rents

B. Gross Annual Rents / Property Price

C. Property Price × Gross Annual Rents

D. Gross Annual Rents × Property Price

Answer: A

The Gross Rent Multiplier (GRM) is calculated by dividing the property price by the gross annual rents.

➡**12. What is the formula for calculating depreciation?**

A. (Cost of the Property - Salvage Value) / Useful Life

B. (Salvage Value - Cost of the Property) / Useful Life

C. Cost of the Property × Salvage Value

D. Salvage Value × Cost of the Property

Answer: A

Depreciation is calculated by subtracting the salvage value from the cost of the property and dividing by its useful life.

➡**13. What does PITI stand for in mortgage calculations?**

A. Principal, Interest, Taxes, Insurance

B. Payment, Interest, Taxes, Insurance

C. Principal, Income, Taxes, Insurance

D. Payment, Income, Taxes, Insurance

Answer: A

PITI stands for Principal, Interest, Taxes, and Insurance, which are the four components of a mortgage payment.

➡14. What is the formula for calculating equity?

A. Market Value - Mortgage Balance

B. Mortgage Balance - Market Value

C. Market Value × Mortgage Balance

D. Mortgage Balance × Market Value

Answer: A

Equity is calculated as the market value of the property minus the mortgage balance.

➡15. What is the formula for calculating net operating income (NOI)?

A. Gross Income - Operating Expenses

B. Operating Expenses - Gross Income

C. Gross Income × Operating Expenses

D. Operating Expenses × Gross Income

Answer: A

Net Operating Income (NOI) is calculated by subtracting operating expenses from gross income.

➡16. What is the formula for calculating the break-even point?

A. Fixed Costs / (Selling Price - Variable Costs)

B. (Selling Price - Variable Costs) / Fixed Costs

C. Fixed Costs × (Selling Price - Variable Costs)

D. (Selling Price - Variable Costs) × Fixed Costs

Answer: A

The break-even point is calculated by dividing fixed costs by the difference between the selling price and variable costs.

➡**17. What is the formula for calculating the internal rate of return (IRR)?**

A. NPV = 0

B. ROI = 100%

C. NPV × ROI

D. ROI × NPV

Answer: A

The internal rate of return (IRR) is the discount rate that makes the net present value (NPV) of all cash flows equal to zero.

➡**18. What is the formula for calculating the price per square foot?**

A. Total Price / Total Square Footage

B. Total Square Footage / Total Price

C. Total Price × Total Square Footage

D. Total Square Footage × Total Price

Answer: A.

The price per square foot is calculated by dividing the total price by the total square footage.

➡**19. What is the formula for calculating the amortization schedule?**

A. $P \times (r(1+r)^n) / ((1+r)^n-1)$

B. $P \times r \times n$

C. $P / r \times n$

D. $P \times n / r$

Answer: A

The formula for calculating the amortization schedule is $P \times (r(1+r)^n) / ((1+r)^n-1)$.

➡20. What is the formula for calculating the future value of an investment?

A. $P \times (1 + r)^n$

B. $P \times (1 - r)^n$

C. $P / (1 + r)^n$

D. $P / (1 - r)^n$

Answer: A

The future value of an investment is calculated as $P \times (1 + r)^n$.

➡21. How do you calculate the Net Operating Income (NOI) for a property?

A. Gross Income - Operating Expenses

B. Gross Income + Operating Expenses

C. Operating Expenses - Gross Income

D. Gross Income $\times$ Operating Expenses

Answer: A

Net Operating Income is calculated by subtracting the operating expenses from the gross income.

➡22. What is the formula for calculating the loan-to-value ratio (LTV)?

A. Mortgage Amount / Appraised Value

B. Appraised Value / Mortgage Amount

C. Mortgage Amount × Appraised Value

D. Appraised Value × Mortgage Amount

Answer: A

The loan-to-value ratio (LTV) is calculated by dividing the mortgage amount by the appraised value of the property.

➡**23. What is the formula for calculating the cash-on-cash return?**

A. Annual Pre-tax Cash Flow / Total Cash Invested

B. Total Cash Invested / Annual Pre-tax Cash Flow

C. Annual Pre-tax Cash Flow × Total Cash Invested

D. Total Cash Invested × Annual Pre-tax Cash Flow

Answer: A

The cash-on-cash return is calculated by dividing the annual pre-tax cash flow by the total cash invested.

➡**24. What is the formula for calculating the debt service coverage ratio (DSCR)?**

A. Net Operating Income / Debt Service

B. Debt Service / Net Operating Income

C. Net Operating Income × Debt Service

D. Debt Service × Net Operating Income

Answer: A

The debt service coverage ratio (DSCR) is calculated by dividing the net operating income by the debt service.

➡**25. What is the formula for calculating the equity build-up rate?**

A. (Principal Paid in Year 1 / Initial Investment) × 100

B. (Initial Investment / Principal Paid in Year 1) × 100

C. Principal Paid in Year 1 × Initial Investment

D. Initial Investment × Principal Paid in Year 1

Answer: A

The equity build-up rate is calculated by dividing the principal paid in the first year by the initial investment and then multiplying by 100.

➡26. What is the formula for calculating the gross operating income (GOI)?

A. Gross Potential Income - Vacancy and Credit Losses

B. Vacancy and Credit Losses - Gross Potential Income

C. Gross Potential Income × Vacancy and Credit Losses

D. Vacancy and Credit Losses × Gross Potential Income

Answer: A

The gross operating income (GOI) is calculated by subtracting vacancy and credit losses from the gross potential income.

➡27. What is the formula for calculating the effective gross income (EGI)?

A. Gross Operating Income + Other Income

B. Other Income - Gross Operating Income

C. Gross Operating Income × Other Income

D. Other Income × Gross Operating Income

Answer: A

The effective gross income (EGI) is calculated by adding other income to the gross operating income.

➡28. What is the formula for calculating the absorption rate?

A. Number of Units Sold / Number of Units Available

B. Number of Units Available / Number of Units Sold

C. Number of Units Sold × Number of Units Available

D. Number of Units Available × Number of Units Sold

Answer: A

The absorption rate is calculated by dividing the number of units sold by the number of units available.

➡29. What is the formula for calculating the price-to-rent ratio?

A. Home Price / Annual Rent

B. Annual Rent / Home Price

C. Home Price × Annual Rent

D. Annual Rent × Home Price

Answer: A

The price-to-rent ratio is calculated by dividing the home price by the annual rent.

➡30. What is the formula for calculating the yield?

A. Annual Income / Investment Cost

B. Investment Cost / Annual Income

C. Annual Income × Investment Cost

D. Investment Cost × Annual Income

Answer: A

The yield is calculated by dividing the annual income by the investment cost.

➡31. What is the formula for calculating the Gross Rent Multiplier (GRM)?

A. Sales Price / Monthly Rent

B. Monthly Rent / Sales Price

C. Sales Price × Monthly Rent

D. Monthly Rent × Sales Price

Answer: A

The Gross Rent Multiplier (GRM) is calculated by dividing the sales price by the monthly rent.

➠**32. How do you calculate the Loan-to-Value ratio (LTV)?**

A. Loan Amount / Appraised Value

B. Appraised Value / Loan Amount

C. Loan Amount × Appraised Value

D. Appraised Value × Loan Amount

Answer: A

The Loan-to-Value ratio (LTV) is calculated by dividing the loan amount by the appraised value of the property.

➠**33. How do you calculate the Net Operating Income (NOI)?**

A. Gross Operating Income - Operating Expenses

B. Operating Expenses - Gross Operating Income

C. Gross Operating Income × Operating Expenses

D. Operating Expenses × Gross Operating Income

Answer: A

The Net Operating Income (NOI) is calculated by subtracting the operating expenses from the gross operating income.

➠**34. How do you calculate the Debt Service Coverage Ratio (DSCR)?**

A. Net Operating Income / Debt Service

B. Debt Service / Net Operating Income

C. Net Operating Income × Debt Service

D. Debt Service × Net Operating Income

Answer: A

The Debt Service Coverage Ratio (DSCR) is calculated by dividing the Net Operating Income by the Debt Service.

➡ **35. What is the formula for calculating the Break-Even Ratio (BER)?**

A. (Operating Expenses + Debt Service) / Gross Operating Income

B. Gross Operating Income / (Operating Expenses + Debt Service)

C. (Operating Expenses + Debt Service) × Gross Operating Income

D. Gross Operating Income × (Operating Expenses + Debt Service)

Answer: A

The Break-Even Ratio (BER) is calculated by dividing the sum of operating expenses and debt service by the gross operating income.

➡ **36. How do you calculate the Effective Gross Income (EGI)?**

A. Gross Income - Vacancy Losses + Other Income

B. Gross Income + Vacancy Losses - Other Income

C. Gross Income × Vacancy Losses + Other Income

D. Gross Income + Vacancy Losses × Other Income

Answer: A

The Effective Gross Income (EGI) is calculated by subtracting vacancy losses from the gross income and adding any other income.

➡ **37. What is the formula for calculating the Operating Expense Ratio (OER)?**

A. Operating Expenses / Effective Gross Income

B. Effective Gross Income / Operating Expenses

C. Operating Expenses × Effective Gross Income

D. Effective Gross Income × Operating Expenses

Answer: A

The Operating Expense Ratio (OER) is calculated by dividing the operating expenses by the effective gross income.

→38. How do you calculate the Cash-on-Cash Return?

A. Cash Flow Before Taxes / Initial Investment

B. Initial Investment / Cash Flow Before Taxes

C. Cash Flow Before Taxes × Initial Investment

D. Initial Investment × Cash Flow Before Taxes

Answer: A

The Cash-on-Cash Return is calculated by dividing the cash flow before taxes by the initial investment.

→39. What is the formula for calculating the Amortization Factor?

A. Monthly Payment / Loan Amount

B. Loan Amount / Monthly Payment

C. Monthly Payment × Loan Amount

D. Loan Amount × Monthly Payment

Answer: A

The Amortization Factor is calculated by dividing the monthly payment by the loan amount.

→40. How do you calculate the Equity Dividend Rate (EDR)?

A. Cash Flow After Taxes / Equity Investment

B. Equity Investment / Cash Flow After Taxes

C. Cash Flow After Taxes × Equity Investment

D. Equity Investment × Cash Flow After Taxes

➠41. What is the formula for calculating the Debt Service Coverage Ratio (DSCR)?

A. Net Operating Income / Debt Service

B. Debt Service / Net Operating Income

C. Net Operating Income × Debt Service

D. Debt Service - Net Operating Income

Answer: A

The Debt Service Coverage Ratio is calculated by dividing the Net Operating Income by the Debt Service.

➠42. How do you calculate the Gross Rent Multiplier (GRM)?

A. Property Price / Monthly Rent

B. Monthly Rent / Property Price

C. Annual Rent / Property Price

D. Property Price / Annual Rent

Answer: A

The Gross Rent Multiplier is calculated by dividing the property price by the monthly rent.

➠43. What is the formula for calculating Loan-to-Value ratio?

A. Loan Amount / Property Value

B. Property Value / Loan Amount

C. Loan Amount × Property Value

D. Property Value - Loan Amount

Answer: A

The Loan-to-Value ratio is calculated by dividing the loan amount by the property value.

➡️44. How do you calculate the break-even point in a real estate investment?

    A. Fixed Costs / (Selling Price - Variable Costs)

    B. (Selling Price - Variable Costs) / Fixed Costs

    C. Fixed Costs × Selling Price

    D. Selling Price / Fixed Costs

Answer: A

The break-even point is calculated by dividing the fixed costs by the difference between the selling price and variable costs.

➡️45. How do you calculate the Return on Investment (ROI) for a property?

    A. (Net Profit / Investment Cost) × 100

    B. (Investment Cost / Net Profit) × 100

    C. Net Profit × Investment Cost

    D. Investment Cost - Net Profit

Answer: A

The Return on Investment is calculated by dividing the net profit by the investment cost and then multiplying by 100.

➡️46. How do you calculate the equity in a property?

    A. Property Value - Mortgage Balance

    B. Mortgage Balance - Property Value

    C. Property Value × Mortgage Balance

    D. Mortgage Balance / Property Value

Answer: A

Equity is calculated by subtracting the mortgage balance from the property value.

➡47. What is the formula for calculating the amortization payment?

  A. Principal Amount / Number of Payments

  B. Interest Rate / Number of Payments

  C. (Principal Amount × Interest Rate) / Number of Payments

  D. (Principal Amount × Interest Rate) / (1 - (1 + Interest Rate)^-Number of Payments)

Answer: D

The amortization payment is calculated using the formula mentioned.

➡48. What is the formula for calculating the Internal Rate of Return (IRR) for a real estate investment?

  A. The discount rate that makes the Net Present Value zero

  B. The rate that equals the Net Operating Income

  C. The rate that equals the Debt Service

  D. The rate that makes the Gross Income zero

Answer: A

The Internal Rate of Return is the discount rate that makes the Net Present Value of all cash flows from a particular investment equal to zero.

➡49. What is the formula for calculating the rate of return on an investment property?

  A. (Net Profit / Cost of Investment) × 100

  B. (Cost of Investment / Net Profit) × 100

  C. Net Profit × Cost of Investment

D. Cost of Investment - Net Profit

Answer: A

The rate of return is calculated by dividing the net profit by the cost of the investment and then multiplying by 100.

➡**50. How do you calculate the net profit from a real estate investment?**

   A. Selling Price - (Buying Price + Costs)

   B. (Buying Price + Costs) - Selling Price

   C. Selling Price × Buying Price

   D. Buying Price / Selling Price

Answer: A

The Net Operating Income (NOI) is calculated by subtracting the operating expenses from the gross operating income.

Specialty Areas

Colorado's diverse landscape and booming economy offer a wide range of specialty areas in real estate. From mountain resorts to urban lofts, the state has something for everyone. This chapter will explore the various specialty areas in Colorado real estate, helping you understand the unique opportunities and challenges each presents.

Residential Real Estate

Single-Family Homes

These are the most common type of residential property, ranging from bungalows to large estates.

Condominiums

Condos offer homeownership with less maintenance, often with added amenities like pools and gyms.

Townhouses

These are multi-floor homes that share one or more walls with adjacent properties but have separate entrances.

Commercial Real Estate

Office Spaces

Colorado's growing tech industry has increased the demand for office spaces, particularly in cities like Denver and Boulder.

Retail Spaces

From shopping malls to boutique stores, retail spaces are a significant part of Colorado's commercial real estate.

Industrial Properties

These include warehouses, factories, and other large facilities, often located in industrial parks.

Vacation and Resort Properties

Ski Resorts

Colorado is home to world-renowned ski resorts like Aspen and Vail, making it a hot market for vacation properties.

Lakefront Properties

Areas like Grand Lake offer stunning lakefront properties, ideal for both vacation and year-round living.

Agricultural and Rural Properties

Farms

Colorado's diverse climate makes it suitable for various types of farming, from cattle ranches to vineyards.

Land

Raw land offers opportunities for development or conservation, depending on the zoning regulations.

Historic and Luxury Properties

Historic Homes

Colorado has a rich history, reflected in its many historic homes, often found in areas like Denver's Capitol Hill.

Luxury Estates

High-end properties offer premium amenities and are often located in exclusive neighborhoods or scenic locations.

Niche Markets

Student Housing

With several universities and colleges, there's a steady demand for student housing, particularly in cities like Boulder and Fort Collins.

Senior Living

Colorado's healthy lifestyle attracts many retirees, creating a market for senior living communities.

Legal and Zoning Considerations

Zoning Laws

Different specialty areas often have specific zoning requirements, such as agricultural, residential, or commercial.

Land Use Regulations

These govern how a property can be used and can significantly impact its value and potential for development.

Market Trends and Investment

Market Analysis

Understanding market trends in different specialty areas can help you make informed investment decisions.

ROI Considerations

Different specialty areas offer varying levels of risk and return on investment.

Conclusion

Colorado's real estate market is as diverse as its landscape, offering a wide range of specialty areas to explore. Whether you're interested in commercial ventures, residential living, or niche markets like student housing or luxury estates, there's something for everyone.

Action Steps for the Reader

1. Identify which specialty areas interest you the most and align with your investment goals or lifestyle preferences.

2. Research the legal and zoning considerations for your chosen specialty area.

3. Conduct a thorough market analysis to understand the risks and potential returns.

By understanding the various specialty areas in Colorado real estate, you'll be better equipped to make informed decisions, whether you're buying, selling, or investing.

Mock Exam Specialty Areas

➡ 1. Which type of real estate is often the entry point for many new agents and brokers?

A. Commercial

B. Industrial

C. Residential

D. Luxury

Answer: C. Residential

Explanation: The chapter states that residential real estate is often the entry point for many new agents and brokers.

➡ 2. What type of property is a penthouse?

A. Industrial

B. Commercial

C. Residential

D. Luxury

Answer: D. Luxury

Explanation: Penthouses are high-end apartments located on the top floors of high-rise buildings and fall under luxury real estate.

➡ 3. What is a key skill required in commercial real estate?

A. Financial Analysis

B. Knowledge of Industrial Machinery

C. Strong Interpersonal Skills

D. Discretion and Confidentiality

Answer: A. Financial Analysis

Explanation: Financial analysis is crucial in commercial real estate for understanding balance sheets, income statements, and cash flow.

➡4. What type of property is a factory?

A. Commercial

B. Industrial

C. Residential

D. Luxury

Answer: B. Industrial

Explanation: Factories are geared towards manufacturing, production, and distribution, which falls under industrial real estate.

➡5. What is a key regulatory aspect in industrial real estate?

A. Luxury tax implications

B. OSHA regulations

C. Fair Housing Laws

D. Commercial zoning laws

Answer: B. OSHA regulations

Explanation: Occupational Safety and Health Administration (OSHA) regulations are key in industrial real estate.

➡6. What type of property is a shopping mall?

A. Commercial

B. Industrial

C. Residential

D. Luxury

Answer: A. Commercial

Explanation: Shopping malls fall under commercial real estate as they are used for business activities.

➡7. **What is a key skill required in luxury real estate?**

A. Financial Analysis

B. Knowledge of Industrial Machinery

C. Strong Interpersonal Skills

D. Discretion and Confidentiality

Answer: D. Discretion and Confidentiality

Explanation: Clients in the luxury sector value their privacy highly, making discretion and confidentiality key skills.

➡8. **What type of property is a townhouse?**

A. Commercial

B. Industrial

C. Residential

D. Luxury

Answer: C. Residential

Explanation: Townhouses are multi-floor homes designed for individual or family living, which falls under residential real estate.

➡9. **What is a key regulatory aspect in residential real estate?**

A. Luxury tax implications

B. OSHA regulations

C. Fair Housing Laws

D. Commercial zoning laws

Answer: C. Fair Housing Laws

Explanation: Fair Housing Laws are key regulatory aspects in residential real estate to ensure equal opportunity in housing.

➡10. **What type of property is a distribution center?**

A. Commercial

B. Industrial

C. Residential

D. Luxury

Answer: B. Industrial

Explanation: Distribution centers are used for storing and distributing goods, which falls under industrial real estate.

➡11. **What type of real estate involves the sale of businesses?**

A. Commercial

B. Business Brokerage

C. Residential

D. Luxury

Answer: B. Business Brokerage

Explanation: Business Brokerage involves the sale of businesses, including their assets and real estate.

➡12. **What is a key skill required in business brokerage?**

A. Negotiation Skills

B. Knowledge of Industrial Machinery

C. Strong Interpersonal Skills

D. Financial Analysis

Answer: A. Negotiation Skills

Explanation: Negotiation skills are crucial in business brokerage to secure the best deals for clients.

➠**13. What type of real estate involves the sale of farmland?**

A. Commercial

B. Industrial

C. Agricultural

D. Luxury

Answer: C. Agricultural

Explanation: Agricultural real estate involves the sale of farmland and agricultural facilities.

➠**14. What is a key regulatory aspect in agricultural real estate?**

A. EPA Regulations

B. OSHA regulations

C. Fair Housing Laws

D. Luxury tax implications

Answer: A. EPA Regulations

Explanation: Environmental Protection Agency (EPA) regulations are key in agricultural real estate.

➡️15. What type of property is a hotel?

A. Commercial

B. Industrial

C. Residential

D. Hospitality

Answer: D. Hospitality

Explanation: Hotels fall under hospitality real estate, which is a sub-category of commercial real estate.

➡️16. What is a key skill required in hospitality real estate?

A. Customer Service

B. Knowledge of Industrial Machinery

C. Strong Interpersonal Skills

D. Financial Analysis

Answer: A. Customer Service

Explanation: Customer service is crucial in hospitality real estate to ensure guest satisfaction.

➡️17. What type of real estate involves the sale of undeveloped land?

A. Commercial

B. Land

C. Residential

D. Luxury

Answer: B. Land

Explanation: The sale of undeveloped land falls under land real estate.

➡️18. What is a key regulatory aspect in land real estate?

A. Zoning Laws

B. OSHA regulations

C. Fair Housing Laws

D. Luxury tax implications

Answer: A. Zoning Laws

Explanation: Zoning laws are key in land real estate to determine the types of development that can occur.

➡️**19. What type of property is a condominium?**

A. Commercial

B. Industrial

C. Residential

D. Luxury

Answer: C. Residential

Explanation: Condominiums are multi-unit properties that are sold individually, which falls under residential real estate.

➡️**20. What is a key skill required in land real estate?**

A. Negotiation Skills

B. Knowledge of Zoning Laws

C. Strong Interpersonal Skills

D. Financial Analysis

Answer: B. Knowledge of Zoning Laws

Explanation: Knowledge of zoning laws is crucial in land real estate to guide clients on permissible uses.

➥21. What is the primary focus of industrial real estate?

   A. Warehouses

   B. Hotels

   C. Farmland

   D. Condominiums

Answer: A. Warehouses

Explanation: Industrial real estate primarily focuses on warehouses and manufacturing buildings.

➥22. What is a 1031 exchange commonly used for?

   A. Residential properties

   B. Commercial properties

   C. Agricultural properties

   D. Industrial properties

Answer: B. Commercial properties

Explanation: A 1031 exchange is commonly used to defer capital gains tax in commercial real estate.

➥23. What is the main consideration in retail real estate?

   A. Location

   B. Size

   C. Zoning

   D. Tax implications

Answer: A. Location

Explanation: Location is the main consideration in retail real estate, as it directly impacts customer footfall.

➡24. What is the primary focus of residential real estate?

A. Single-family homes

B. Warehouses

C. Hotels

D. Farmland

Answer: A. Single-family homes

Explanation: Residential real estate primarily focuses on single-family homes, although it can include multi-family units.

➡25. What is the main consideration in luxury real estate?

A. Price

B. Location

C. Amenities

D. Size

Answer: C. Amenities

Explanation: Luxury real estate often focuses on the amenities offered, such as pools, gyms, and concierge services.

➡26. What is the primary advantage of investing in mixed-use real estate?

A. Diversification

B. Lower taxes

C. Easier management

D. Higher rent

Answer: A. Diversification

Explanation: Mixed-use real estate offers diversification as it combines residential, commercial, and sometimes industrial spaces.

➡27. What is the main disadvantage of investing in vacation real estate?

   A. Seasonal income

   B. High maintenance

   C. Zoning restrictions

   D. High taxes

Answer: **A. Seasonal income**

Explanation: **Vacation real estate often has seasonal income, which can be a disadvantage for consistent cash flow.**

➡28. What is the primary consideration when investing in student housing?

   A. Proximity to educational institutions

   B. Luxury amenities

   C. Tax benefits

   D. Size of the property

Answer: **A. Proximity to educational institutions**

Explanation: **The primary consideration for student housing is its proximity to educational institutions.**

➡29. What is the main benefit of investing in senior living communities?

   A. Lower maintenance

   B. Steady income

   C. Tax benefits

   D. High rent

Answer: **B. Steady income**

Explanation: **Senior living communities often provide a steady income due to long-term leases.**

➡30. What is a triple net lease commonly used in?

A. Residential properties

B. Commercial properties

C. Industrial properties

D. Agricultural properties

Answer: B. Commercial properties

Explanation: A triple net lease is commonly used in commercial real estate, where the tenant pays property taxes, insurance, and maintenance costs.

➡31. What is the primary focus of hospitality real estate?

A. Hotels and resorts

B. Warehouses

C. Office buildings

D. Farmland

Answer: A. Hotels and resorts

Explanation: Hospitality real estate primarily focuses on hotels, resorts, and other lodging options.

➡32. What is the main consideration in agricultural real estate?

A. Soil quality

B. Location

C. Size

D. Zoning

Answer: A. Soil quality

Explanation: Soil quality is the main consideration in agricultural real estate for farming purposes.

➡33. What is the primary advantage of investing in REITs?

A. Liquidity

B. Control over property

C. Tax benefits

D. High rent

Answer: A. Liquidity

Explanation: REITs offer liquidity as they can be easily bought and sold on stock exchanges.

➡34. What is the main disadvantage of investing in office real estate?

A. High vacancy rates

B. Seasonal income

C. Zoning restrictions

D. High maintenance

Answer: A. High vacancy rates

Explanation: Office real estate can have high vacancy rates, especially in economic downturns.

➡35. What is the primary focus of mobile home parks?

A. Affordable housing

B. Luxury living

C. Commercial spaces

D. Agricultural land

Answer: A. Affordable housing

Explanation: Mobile home parks primarily focus on providing affordable housing options.

➡36. What is the primary consideration when investing in retail real estate?

A. Foot traffic

B. Tax benefits

C. Size of the property

D. Proximity to educational institutions

Answer: A. Foot traffic

Explanation: Foot traffic is crucial for the success of retail real estate.

➡37. What is the main benefit of investing in industrial real estate?

A. High rent

B. Long-term leases

C. Seasonal income

D. Tax benefits

Answer: B. Long-term leases

Explanation: Industrial real estate often comes with long-term leases, providing stable income.

➡38. What is a common disadvantage of investing in multi-family properties?

A. High maintenance costs

B. Low rent

C. Zoning restrictions

D. Seasonal income

Answer: A. High maintenance costs

Explanation: Multi-family properties often have higher maintenance costs due to multiple units.

➥39. What is the primary focus of medical real estate?

A. Hospitals and clinics

B. Office buildings

C. Warehouses

D. Hotels and resorts

Answer: A. Hospitals and clinics

Explanation: Medical real estate primarily focuses on hospitals, clinics, and other healthcare facilities.

➥40. What is the main consideration in raw land investment?

A. Zoning restrictions

B. Soil quality

C. Location

D. Size

Answer: C. Location

Explanation: Location is key in raw land investment for future development.

➥41. What is the primary advantage of investing in storage units?

A. Low maintenance

B. High rent

C. Tax benefits

D. Seasonal income

Answer: A. Low maintenance

Explanation: Storage units generally require low maintenance.

➡42. What is the main disadvantage of investing in co-working spaces?

A. High vacancy rates

B. Low rent

C. Zoning restrictions

D. Seasonal income

Answer: A. High vacancy rates

Explanation: Co-working spaces can have high vacancy rates, especially during economic downturns.

➡43. What is the primary focus of green real estate?

A. Energy efficiency

B. High rent

C. Tax benefits

D. Size of the property

Answer: A. Energy efficiency

Explanation: Green real estate primarily focuses on energy-efficient buildings.

➡44. What is the main benefit of investing in brownfield sites?

A. Tax incentives

B. High rent

C. Seasonal income

D. Long-term leases

Answer: A. Tax incentives

Explanation: Brownfield sites often come with tax incentives for redevelopment.

➡ 45. What is the primary consideration when investing in infill real estate?

A. Location

B. Size

C. Zoning restrictions

D. Soil quality

Answer: A. Location

Explanation: Infill real estate focuses on developing vacant or underused parcels within existing urban areas, so location is key.

➡ 46. What is the main disadvantage of investing in luxury real estate?

A. High maintenance costs

B. Seasonal income

C. Zoning restrictions

D. Low rent

Answer: A. High maintenance costs

Explanation: Luxury real estate often comes with high maintenance costs.

➡ 47. What is the primary focus of transit-oriented development?

A. Proximity to public transport

B. Luxury amenities

C. Tax benefits

D. Size of the property

Answer: A. Proximity to public transport

Explanation: Transit-oriented development focuses on properties close to public transport facilities.

→48. What is the main benefit of investing in adaptive reuse properties?

A. Tax incentives

B. High rent

C. Seasonal income

D. Long-term leases

Answer: A. Tax incentives

Explanation: Adaptive reuse properties often come with tax incentives for redevelopment.

→49. What is the primary consideration when investing in distressed properties?

A. Cost of renovation

B. Location

C. Size

D. Zoning

Answer: A. Cost of renovation

Explanation: The cost of renovation is a key consideration when investing in distressed properties.

→50. What is the main disadvantage of investing in fixer-uppers?

A. High renovation costs

B. Low rent

C. Zoning restrictions

D. Seasonal income

Answer: A. High renovation costs

Explanation: Fixer-uppers often come with high renovation costs that can eat into profits.

Ethics and Legal Considerations

Ethics and legal considerations are the pillars that uphold the integrity of the real estate industry. This chapter aims to provide a comprehensive guide on the ethical and legal landscape in Colorado real estate, helping you navigate the complexities with confidence.

Ethical Guidelines

Code of Ethics

The National Association of Realtors (NAR) has a Code of Ethics that all Realtors are expected to follow. This code includes duties to clients, the public, and other Realtors.

State-Specific Guidelines

Colorado has its own set of ethical guidelines that complement the NAR Code of Ethics, focusing on issues like discrimination and fiduciary duties.

Ethical Dilemmas

Real estate professionals often face ethical dilemmas, such as dual agency or conflicts of interest. It's crucial to handle these situations with integrity.

Legal Framework

Licensing Laws

Colorado has specific laws governing the licensing of real estate agents, including educational requirements and background checks.

Contract Laws

Contracts form the legal basis of any real estate transaction. Understanding the elements that make a contract legally binding is essential.

Property Laws

These laws govern property ownership, land use, and tenant rights, among other things.

Fair Housing and Anti-Discrimination Laws

Federal Laws

The Fair Housing Act prohibits discrimination based on race, color, religion, sex, disability, familial status, or national origin.

Colorado Laws

Colorado's anti-discrimination laws are even more extensive, adding protections for sexual orientation, marital status, and military status.

Disclosure Requirements

Seller's Property Disclosure

Colorado law requires sellers to provide a comprehensive disclosure form, detailing the condition of the property.

Lead-Based Paint Disclosure

Federal law mandates this disclosure for homes built before 1978.

Agency Disclosure

Colorado requires agents to disclose their agency relationships clearly, whether they represent the buyer, the seller, or both.

Legal Issues and Disputes

Breach of Contract

When a party fails to fulfill their contractual obligations, legal remedies may include monetary damages or specific performance.

Property Disputes

These can range from boundary issues to disputes over easements or water rights.

Professional Liability

Real estate professionals can be held liable for negligence, misrepresentation, or breach of fiduciary duties.

Risk Management

Insurance

Professional liability insurance, also known as Errors and Omissions (E&O) insurance, can protect against legal claims.

Continuing Education

Colorado requires ongoing education for real estate professionals, often including courses on ethics and legal considerations.

Conclusion

Ethics and legal considerations are not just guidelines but essential practices that ensure the integrity and professionalism of the real estate industry in Colorado.

Action Steps for the Reader

1. Familiarize yourself with both the NAR Code of Ethics and Colorado's specific ethical guidelines.
2. Understand the legal framework governing real estate in Colorado, including licensing, contract, and property laws.
3. Be aware of the state's disclosure requirements and anti-discrimination laws.

By understanding the ethical and legal landscape, you'll be better equipped to navigate the complexities of the Colorado real estate market successfully.

Mock Exam Ethics and Legal Considerations

➡1. **What are the three main categories of the NAR Code of Ethics?**

A. Duties to Clients, Duties to Realtors, Duties to the Public

B. Duties to Clients and Customers, Duties to the Public, Duties to Realtors

C. Duties to Sellers, Duties to Buyers, Duties to the Public

D. Duties to the Government, Duties to Clients, Duties to Realtors

Answer: B

The NAR Code of Ethics is divided into three main categories: **Duties to Clients and Customers, Duties to the Public, and Duties to Realtors.**

➡2. **Which of the following is NOT a fiduciary duty?**

A. Loyalty

B. Confidentiality

C. Manipulation

D. Full Disclosure

Answer: C

Manipulation is not a fiduciary duty. The fiduciary duties are loyalty, confidentiality, obedience, reasonable care, accounting, and full disclosure.

➡3. **What is the primary purpose of zoning laws?**

A. To increase property taxes

B. To regulate land use

C. To protect endangered species

D. To promote business

Answer: B

The primary purpose of zoning laws is to regulate land use, such as residential, commercial, or industrial zones.

➡4. What does 'reasonable care' in fiduciary duties imply?

A. Taking vacations regularly

B. Staying updated on market trends

C. Investing in real estate

D. Focusing on commission

Answer: B

'Reasonable care' means staying updated on market trends, legal changes, and other factors that could affect a client's decision.

➡5. What is the consequence of not adhering to full disclosure?

A. Increased commission

B. Legal repercussions

C. More clients

D. Promotion

Answer: B

Failing to adhere to full disclosure can lead to legal repercussions, including lawsuits and loss of license.

➡6. Which federal law is designed to ensure fair housing?

A. The Sherman Act

B. The Fair Housing Act

C. The Clayton Act

D. The Dodd-Frank Act

Answer: B

The Fair Housing Act is designed to prevent discrimination in housing based on race, color, religion, sex, or national origin.

➡️7. What is the minimum age requirement for obtaining a real estate license in most states?

A. 16

B. 18

C. 21

D. 25

Answer: B

The minimum age requirement for obtaining a real estate license in most states is 18 years.

➡️8. What is the key to resolving ethical dilemmas like dual agency?

A. Ignoring the issue

B. Full disclosure and informed consent

C. Choosing one party to represent

D. Consulting a lawyer

Answer: B

The key to resolving ethical dilemmas like dual agency lies in full disclosure and obtaining informed consent from all parties involved.

➡️9. Which of the following is NOT an element that makes a contract legally binding?

A. Offer and acceptance

B. Consideration

C. Coercion

D. Legality of purpose

Answer: C

Coercion is not an element that makes a contract legally binding. A contract must have offer and acceptance, consideration, and legality of purpose to be legally binding.

➡10. **What does the NAR Code of Ethics say about advertising?**

A. It encourages aggressive advertising

B. It prohibits all forms of advertising

C. It requires truthful advertising

D. It promotes online advertising only

Answer: C

The NAR Code of Ethics requires that all advertising be truthful and not misleading.

➡11. **What is the primary role of the Real Estate Commission in most states?**

A. To sell properties

B. To regulate and license real estate agents

C. To build homes

D. To provide loans

Answer: B

The primary role of the Real Estate Commission in most states is to regulate and license real estate agents.

➡12. **What is the statute of frauds?**

A. A law that requires certain contracts to be in writing

B. A law that allows fraud in certain cases

C. A law that regulates online advertising

D. A law that deals with zoning issues

Answer: A

The statute of frauds is a law that requires certain contracts, like those for the sale of real estate, to be in writing to be enforceable.

➡**13. What does RESPA stand for?**

A. Real Estate Settlement Procedures Act

B. Real Estate Sales Professional Act

C. Residential Sales Property Act

D. Real Estate Security Policy Act

Answer: A

RESPA stands for Real Estate Settlement Procedures Act, which aims to provide transparency in the home buying process.

➡**14. What is puffing in real estate terms?**

A. Illegal misrepresentation

B. Exaggeration of property features

C. Accurate description of property

D. Undervaluing a property

Answer: B

Puffing refers to the exaggeration of property features, which is generally considered legal but can be ethically questionable.

➡**15. What is the primary purpose of an escrow account?**

A. To hold funds for investment

B. To hold funds until the completion of a real estate transaction

C. To pay for the agent's commission

D. To pay property taxes

Answer: B

The primary purpose of an escrow account is to hold funds until the completion of a real estate transaction.

➠16. What does the term "redlining" refer to?

A. Drawing property boundaries

B. Discriminatory lending practices

C. Marking properties for demolition

D. Highlighting important clauses in a contract

Answer: B

Redlining refers to discriminatory lending practices that deny loans or insurance to people based on their location, often targeting minority communities.

➠17. What is the difference between ethics and laws?

A. Ethics are legally binding, laws are not

B. Laws are legally binding, ethics are not

C. Ethics and laws are the same

D. Laws are optional, ethics are mandatory

Answer: B

Laws are legally binding rules that must be followed, while ethics are moral principles that guide behavior but are not legally enforceable.

→18. What is the "doctrine of caveat emptor"?

A. Let the buyer beware

B. Let the seller beware

C. Buyer's premium

D. Seller's advantage

Answer: A

The doctrine of "caveat emptor" means "let the buyer beware," indicating that the buyer is responsible for due diligence.

→19. What is a bilateral contract?

A. A contract with only one party

B. A contract with two parties

C. A contract with multiple parties

D. A contract that is not legally binding

Answer: B

A bilateral contract is a contract involving two parties where each party has made a promise to the other.

→20. What is the role of a title company?

A. To market properties

B. To ensure the title is clear and prepare for its transfer

C. To provide loans

D. To build homes

Answer: B

The role of a title company is to ensure that the title to a piece of real estate is legitimate and to prepare for its transfer from the seller to the buyer.

➡ **21. What is the "dual agency" in real estate?**

A. When an agent represents both the buyer and the seller

B. When two agents work for the same client

C. When an agent works for two different real estate firms

D. When an agent sells both commercial and residential properties

Answer: A

Dual agency occurs when a real estate agent represents both the buyer and the seller in the same transaction.

➡ **22. What does the Fair Housing Act prohibit?**

A. Discrimination based on race, color, religion, sex, or national origin

B. All forms of discrimination

C. Discrimination based on financial status

D. Discrimination based on occupation

Answer: A

The Fair Housing Act prohibits discrimination in housing based on race, color, religion, sex, or national origin.

➡ **23. What is earnest money?**

A. Money paid by the buyer at the time of the property closing

B. A refundable deposit

C. Money paid by the buyer to show serious intent to purchase

D. Money paid by the seller as a part of the listing agreement

Answer: C

Earnest money is money paid by the buyer to show serious intent to purchase the property.

➡ **24. What is a contingency in a real estate contract?**

   A. A binding clause

   B. A non-negotiable term

   C. A condition that must be met for the contract to be binding

   D. A penalty for breach of contract

Answer: C

A contingency is a condition that must be met for the contract to be binding, such as a home inspection.

➡ **25. What is a fiduciary duty?**

   A. A legal obligation to act in the best interest of another

   B. A duty to find the best property for a client

   C. A duty to sell a property as quickly as possible

   D. A duty to maximize profit

Answer: A

A fiduciary duty is a legal obligation to act in the best interest of another, such as a client.

➡ **26. What is a unilateral contract?**

   A. A contract where only one party makes a promise

   B. A contract where both parties make promises

   C. A contract that involves more than two parties

   D. A contract that is not legally binding

Answer: A

A unilateral contract is a contract where only one party makes a promise, and the other has the option to complete the action.

➡ **27. What is the purpose of a disclosure statement?**

A. To disclose the agent's commission

B. To disclose any known defects or issues with the property

C. To disclose the buyer's financial status

D. To disclose the terms of the mortgage

Answer: B

The purpose of a disclosure statement is to disclose any known defects or issues with the property to the buyer.

➡ **28. What does "time is of the essence" mean in a real estate contract?**

A. Deadlines must be strictly adhered to

B. Time limits are flexible

C. The contract has no expiration date

D. The contract can be terminated at any time

Answer: A

"Time is of the essence" means that deadlines set forth in the contract must be strictly adhered to.

➡ **29. What is a quitclaim deed?**

A. A deed that transfers property with no warranties

B. A deed that includes warranties

C. A deed that transfers leasehold interest

D. A deed that can be easily revoked

Answer: A

A quitclaim deed is a deed that transfers property with no warranties or guarantees.

➡️**30. What is the role of a notary public in a real estate transaction?**

A. To negotiate the terms

B. To verify the identity of the parties and witness the signing of documents

C. To provide legal advice

D. To inspect the property

Answer: B

The role of a notary public is to verify the identity of the parties and witness the signing of important documents.

➡️**31. What is the primary purpose of a title search?**

A. To determine the property's market value

B. To verify the legal owner of the property

C. To inspect the condition of the property

D. To assess property taxes

Answer: B

The primary purpose of a title search is to verify the legal owner of the property and ensure there are no liens or other encumbrances.

➡️**32. What is a "balloon payment" in a mortgage?**

A. A small initial payment

B. A large final payment

C. A regular monthly payment

D. An extra payment to reduce interest

Answer: B

A balloon payment is a large final payment at the end of a loan term, usually after a series of smaller payments.

➡33. What is the "right of first refusal" in real estate?

A. The right to refuse a sale

B. The right to be the first to purchase a property before the owner sells it to another party

C. The right to refuse to pay rent

D. The right to refuse a home inspection

Answer: B

The right of first refusal allows an individual or entity the opportunity to purchase a property before the owner sells it to another party.

➡34. What is a "listing agreement"?

A. An agreement between buyer and seller

B. An agreement between a seller and a real estate agent

C. An agreement between a buyer and a real estate agent

D. An agreement between two real estate agents

Answer: B

A listing agreement is a contract between a seller and a real estate agent outlining the terms under which the agent will sell the property.

➡35. What does "under contract" mean in real estate?

A. The property is being appraised

B. The property is being inspected

C. An offer on the property has been accepted, but the sale is not yet complete

D. The property has been sold

Answer: C

"Under contract" means that an offer on the property has been accepted, but the sale is not yet complete, pending contingencies or other terms.

➥36. What is the role of a fiduciary in a real estate transaction?

   A. To act in the best interest of the client

   B. To maximize profits for the brokerage

   C. To represent both buyer and seller equally

   D. To ensure the property passes inspection

Answer: A

The role of a fiduciary is to act in the best interest of the client, whether that's the buyer or the seller.

➥37. What does "escrow" refer to in real estate?

   A. A type of mortgage loan

   B. A neutral third party holding funds or documents until conditions are met

   C. A binding contract between buyer and seller

   D. A home inspection report

Answer: B

Escrow refers to a neutral third party holding funds or documents until certain conditions are met in a real estate transaction.

➥38. What is a "contingency" in a real estate contract?

   A. A penalty for late payment

   B. A condition that must be met for the contract to proceed

   C. An optional add-on to the property

D. A mandatory fee paid to the real estate agent

Answer: B

A contingency is a condition that must be met for the contract to proceed, such as a successful home inspection.

→39. What does "amortization" mean in the context of a mortgage?

A. The process of increasing the loan amount

B. The process of paying off the loan over time

C. The process of adjusting the interest rate

D. The process of transferring the loan to another lender

Answer: B

Amortization is the process of paying off a loan over time through regular payments.

→40. What is "due diligence" in real estate?

A. The responsibility to investigate a property before purchase

B. The obligation to pay property taxes

C. The requirement to obtain a mortgage pre-approval

D. The duty to disclose all known defects to a buyer

Answer: A

Due diligence is the responsibility of the buyer to investigate a property thoroughly before completing the purchase.

→41. What is "redlining" in the context of real estate?

A. Drawing property boundaries

B. Discriminatory practice affecting mortgage availability

C. A type of home inspection

D. A negotiation strategy

Answer: B

Redlining is a discriminatory practice where mortgage lenders deny loans or insurance to certain areas based on racial or ethnic composition.

➠42. **What does "title insurance" protect against?**

A. Property damage

B. Mortgage default

C. Legal claims against property ownership

D. Loss of rental income

Answer: C

Title insurance protects against legal claims challenging the ownership of the property.

➠43. **What is "dual agency" in real estate?**

A. When an agent represents both the buyer and the seller

B. When two agents from the same brokerage represent the buyer and the seller

C. When an agent represents two buyers for the same property

D. When an agent represents two sellers for different properties

Answer: A

Dual agency occurs when a real estate agent represents both the buyer and the seller in the same transaction. This can create a conflict of interest and is illegal in some states.

➠44. **What is a "balloon mortgage"?**

A. A mortgage with fluctuating interest rates

B. A mortgage that requires a large final payment

C. A mortgage with no down payment

D. A mortgage paid off in less than 5 years

Answer: B

A balloon mortgage requires a large final payment at the end of the loan term.

➡45. What is "blockbusting"?

A. Building multiple properties in a short time

B. Encouraging people to sell their homes by instigating fear of a changing neighborhood

C. The process of rezoning land

D. Buying large blocks of property for development

Answer: B

Blockbusting is the practice of encouraging people to sell their homes by instigating fear, often related to racial, ethnic, or social change in a neighborhood.

➡46. What is a "1031 exchange"?

A. A tax-deferred property exchange

B. A type of mortgage loan

C. A property auction

D. An open house event

Answer: A

A 1031 exchange allows the owner to sell a property and reinvest the proceeds in a new property while deferring capital gains tax.

➡47. What is "eminent domain"?

A. The right of the government to acquire private property for public use

B. The highest legal ownership of property

C. A type of zoning regulation

D. A clause in a mortgage contract

Answer: A

Eminent domain is the right of the government to acquire private property for public use, usually with compensation.

➡48. What is "equity" in real estate?

A. The market value of a property

B. The difference between the property's market value and the remaining mortgage balance

C. The initial down payment

D. The annual property tax

Answer: B

Equity is the difference between the market value of the property and the remaining balance on any loans secured by the property.

➡49. What is "escrow" in a real estate transaction?

A. A legal arrangement where a third party holds funds or documents

B. The initial offer made by a buyer

C. The final stage of mortgage approval

D. A type of home inspection

Answer: A

Escrow is a legal arrangement in which a third party temporarily holds funds or documents until the conditions of a contract are met.

➡50. What is "net operating income" in real estate investment?

A. Gross income minus operating expenses

B. Gross income plus operating expenses

C. Mortgage payments minus rental income

D. Property value minus mortgage balance

Answer: A

Net operating income is the gross income generated by a property minus the operating expenses, not including mortgage payments or taxes.

Day of the Exam

The day of the real estate exam is a pivotal moment in your journey to becoming a licensed real estate professional in Colorado. This chapter aims to provide you with a comprehensive guide on what to expect and how to prepare for the day of the exam.

Before the Exam Day

Final Review

In the days leading up to the exam, focus on reviewing key concepts, laws, and calculations. Use flashcards, practice exams, and other study tools to reinforce your knowledge.

Gather Required Documents

Make sure you have all the necessary identification and authorization documents ready. This usually includes a government-issued ID and your exam authorization letter.

Plan Your Route

Know the location of the exam center and how to get there. Plan to arrive at least 30 minutes early to account for any unexpected delays.

On the Exam Day

What to Bring

- Government-issued ID
- Exam authorization letter
- Basic calculator (if allowed)

- Water and a light snack

What Not to Bring

- Electronic devices
- Notes or study materials
- Large bags or backpacks

Dress Code

Dress comfortably but professionally. Layers are advisable as exam rooms can vary in temperature.

At the Exam Center

Check-In Process

Upon arrival, you'll need to check in. Be prepared to show your ID and authorization letter. You may also be asked to store your belongings in a designated area.

Exam Room Rules

Listen carefully to the proctor's instructions and follow all exam room rules. This may include no talking, no leaving the room without permission, and no use of unauthorized materials.

Taking the Exam

Types of Questions

The exam will consist of multiple-choice questions covering various topics like property laws, contracts, and ethics.

Time Management

You'll have a limited amount of time to complete the exam. Use your time wisely, skipping questions you're unsure about and returning to them later.

Marking Answers

Read each question carefully and mark your answers clearly. If you're unsure, make an educated guess; there's no penalty for guessing.

Conclusion

The day of the exam is a culmination of your hard work and preparation. By knowing what to expect and how to prepare, you can approach it with confidence and poise.

Action Steps for the Reader

1. Make a checklist of items to bring and tasks to complete before the exam day.
2. Develop a time management strategy for the exam.
3. Familiarize yourself with the exam center's rules and procedures.

By following these guidelines, you'll be well-prepared to succeed on the day of your Colorado real estate exam.

After the Exam: Next Steps

Congratulations on completing your Colorado real estate exam! Whether you've passed or need to retake the test, this chapter will guide you through the next steps in your real estate journey.

If You've Passed

Celebrate Your Achievement

Take a moment to celebrate your hard work and dedication. Passing the real estate exam is a significant milestone.

Receive Your License

After passing the exam, you'll need to complete any remaining paperwork and pay the licensing fee to receive your official Colorado real estate license.

Join a Brokerage

As a newly licensed agent, you'll need to join a brokerage to start practicing. Research different brokerages to find one that aligns with your career goals.

Continuing Education

Colorado requires real estate professionals to complete continuing education courses. Make sure to understand the requirements and deadlines.

If You Didn't Pass

Review Your Score Report

You'll receive a score report detailing your performance. Use this to identify areas where you need improvement.

Reschedule the Exam

You can usually reschedule the exam after a waiting period. Use this time to focus on your weak areas.

Consider a Tutor or Prep Course

If you're struggling with specific topics, consider hiring a tutor or enrolling in a prep course.

Building Your Career

Networking

Start building your professional network by attending industry events, joining real estate associations, and connecting with mentors.

Marketing Yourself

Develop a marketing plan that includes both online and offline strategies. Consider building a website, leveraging social media, and using traditional marketing methods like flyers and postcards.

Specialization

As you gain experience, consider specializing in a particular area of real estate, such as commercial properties, luxury homes, or property management.

Legal and Ethical Responsibilities

Errors and Omissions Insurance

It's advisable to get Errors and Omissions (E&O) insurance to protect yourself from legal claims related to your professional services.

Code of Ethics

Always adhere to the National Association of Realtors (NAR) Code of Ethics and Colorado's specific ethical guidelines.

Legal Updates

Stay updated on any changes in real estate laws and regulations. Ignorance of the law is not an excuse for breaking it.

Financial Planning

Commission Structure

Understand the commission structure at your brokerage. This will help you set realistic financial goals.

Taxes

As a real estate agent, you're considered an independent contractor. Make sure to set aside money for taxes and consult a tax advisor for specific guidance.

Retirement Planning

Consider setting up a retirement savings plan. Many real estate agents opt for a Solo 401(k) or a SEP IRA.

Conclusion

The journey doesn't end with passing the exam; it's just the beginning. Whether you've passed or need to retake the test, there are clear paths forward.

Action Steps for the Reader

1. Complete any remaining licensing requirements and join a brokerage.

2. Develop a career plan that includes networking, marketing, and specialization.

3. Stay updated on legal and ethical responsibilities, and make sound financial plans.

By following these next steps, you'll be well on your way to a successful career in Colorado real estate.

Career Development

Career development is an ongoing process that doesn't stop once you've obtained your real estate license. This chapter will guide you through the various stages and opportunities for career growth in the Colorado real estate industry.

Setting Career Goals

Short-Term Goals

These could range from closing your first sale to joining a top brokerage within your first year. Be specific and realistic.

Long-Term Goals

Think about where you see yourself in 5, 10, or even 20 years. Do you want to own a brokerage, specialize in luxury real estate, or perhaps venture into property development?

SMART Goals

Use the SMART framework (Specific, Measurable, Achievable, Relevant, Time-bound) to set actionable goals.

Skill Development

Sales Skills

Mastering the art of selling is crucial. This includes understanding client needs, effective communication, and closing deals.

Technical Skills

Learn how to use real estate software, CRM systems, and other tech tools that can make your job easier and more efficient.

Soft Skills

Emotional intelligence, negotiation skills, and problem-solving are just as important as technical know-how.

Networking

Industry Events

Attend real estate conferences, seminars, and workshops to meet industry professionals and learn about the latest trends.

Social Media

Use platforms like LinkedIn, Twitter, and Instagram to connect with peers, clients, and industry leaders.

Mentorship

Find a mentor who can guide you through the complexities of the real estate business.

Joining Professional Organizations

National Association of Realtors (NAR)

Membership offers numerous benefits, including access to exclusive market data and educational resources.

Colorado Association of Realtors

Join your state association for localized support, including legal resources and lobbying efforts.

Specialized Groups

Consider joining groups that focus on your area of interest, such as commercial real estate or property management.

Advanced Certifications and Designations

Certified Residential Specialist (CRS)

This certification is for those specializing in residential real estate.

Accredited Buyer's Representative (ABR)

This designation is ideal for agents who wish to focus on representing buyers.

Broker's License

Obtaining a broker's license allows you to operate your own brokerage and hire other agents.

Financial Planning for Career Growth

Diversifying Income Streams

Don't rely solely on commissions. Consider other income streams like property management fees or real estate investments.

Retirement Planning

As mentioned in the previous chapter, setting up a retirement plan is crucial for long-term financial security.

Business Expenses

Keep track of your expenses, including marketing costs, travel, and any fees associated with maintaining your license or memberships.

Conclusion

Career development in real estate is a continuous journey filled with opportunities for growth and specialization. By setting clear goals, developing essential skills, and taking advantage of educational and networking opportunities, you can build a rewarding and successful career in Colorado real estate.

Action Steps for the Reader

1. Set short-term and long-term career goals using the SMART framework.

2. Identify key skills you need to develop and find resources or courses to improve them.

3. Consider joining professional organizations and obtaining advanced certifications to enhance your credibility and marketability.

By following these guidelines, you're setting the stage for a fulfilling and lucrative career in Colorado real estate.

Conclusion

As you reach the end of this book, take a moment to reflect on the journey you've embarked upon. The path to becoming a licensed real estate professional in Colorado is filled with challenges, but it's also ripe with opportunities. You've armed yourself with knowledge, from understanding the Colorado real estate market to preparing for the exam and planning your career development. This book aimed to be your comprehensive guide, and we hope it has served you well.

The Importance of Continuous Learning

Real estate is an ever-evolving field. Laws change, market trends shift, and new technologies emerge. Continuous learning is not just a requirement for maintaining your license; it's a necessity for staying competitive and providing the best service to your clients. Make a commitment to lifelong learning, whether it's through formal education, self-study, or practical experience.

Networking and Mentorship

Remember, you're not alone on this journey. The importance of networking and mentorship cannot be overstated. The relationships you build today could lead to partnerships, referrals, and opportunities down the line. Attend industry events, join professional organizations, and don't hesitate to seek advice from those who have walked the path before you.

Ethics and Professionalism

Your reputation is your most valuable asset. Always adhere to the highest ethical standards and professional conduct. This not only builds trust with your clients but also sets you apart in a competitive market. The chapters on ethics and legal considerations provide a foundation, but it's up to you to carry those principles into your daily practice.

Financial Planning and Career Growth

As you progress in your career, financial planning becomes increasingly important. From understanding commission structures to planning for retirement, make informed decisions that will contribute to your long-term success. Your career goals may evolve over time, and that's okay. What's important is that you have a plan and the flexibility to adapt.

Final Words

As you close this book, remember that your journey is just beginning. The real estate exam is a significant milestone, but it's not the destination. Whether you're entering the field to revolutionize it or to make a meaningful impact in your community, the potential is limitless.

Action Steps for the Reader

Review and Reflect: Go back to the chapters that you found most challenging and review the key points.

Set Your Goals: Write down your short-term and long-term goals and the steps you'll take to achieve them.

Stay Updated: Subscribe to industry publications, blogs, and forums to keep yourself updated.

Join a Community: Whether online or in person, join a community of real estate professionals for support and guidance.

Thank you for choosing "Colorado Real Estate License Exam: Best Test Prep Book to Help You Get Your License!" as your guide. We wish you all the best in your real estate journey in Colorado.

Made in the USA
Thornton, CO
01/01/25 21:00:36

b54d4603-4d23-4e1a-83d6-7dfc9fbb8085R01